death from alcohol withdrawal—deeply impacted Geller, who has struggled with her own vulnerabilities in the wake of her mother's actions. Geller does not settle into the mire, though she shares her own experiences with remarkable candor. Instead, she brings a professional objectivity to the narrative and illustrates how the threads of addiction can weave through generations. . . . The deliberate nature of Geller's connection with the Navajo Nation also becomes apparent. She participates in Navajo weaving workshops, a palpably symbolic action. Hers is not an easy connection, but it is an enduring one. . . . Interspersed across the pages of the book are images of the actual contents of [a] suitcase, including children's drawings, photos of Geller as a child, and pictures of her parents and her sister. The camera captured smiles and laughter—the faint promise of hope. Geller never lets go of that light."　　　　　　　　　　　　　　　　　　　　—*The Christian Science Monitor*

"*Dog Flowers* by Danielle Geller is a journey story we've never read before. Geller travels through snippets of her own life and that of her mother's, creating a narrative where all roads lead to her mother's homeland on the Navajo Nation. An honest, intimate, and heart-wrenching memoir, it explores a fractured family, the damaging effects of alcoholism and poverty, and what it means to seek healing from legacies of trauma. This book gave me chills. Trained as a librarian and archivist, Geller has created a type of archive, a living collection of memories and documents that speak to a life that is at once precisely individualistic while also being universally resonant. Read this book."　　　　　　—KALI FAJARDO-ANSTINE, author of *Sabrina & Corina*

"*Dog Flowers* pulls the few remaining threads of an unraveled family life. This courageous, honest, desperate, tender, and compelling book tells a daughter's story of her troubled mother. In *Dog Flowers*, we learn that a handful of threads can never reweave the blanket of family or patch up what a mother's abandonment has torn. What little we learn of Geller's Navajo mother comes from collaged notes and journal entries, photographs and reportage—it's a story full of gaps. Which is exactly what's remarkable about this book: Geller does not seek to make anything whole but herself. She refuses to deal in the tropes of redemption and reconciliation—which just shows how much strength it takes not to judge another's life or lie about it. Even her return to her mother's Navajo Nation does not bring about an easy cultural reunion, although it does give us a satisfying sense that while an immediate family can fall apart, an extended family, a tribe, ties a tight web that might just hold."　　　　　　　　　　—HEID E. ERDRICH, poet, author, and editor of the award-winning *New Poets of Native Nations*

Dog Flowers

DOG FLOWERS

A MEMOIR, AN ARCHIVE

Danielle Geller

ONE WORLD
New York

2022 One World Trade Paperback Edition

Published in the United States by One World, an imprint
of Random House, a division of Penguin Random House LLC,
New York.

ONE WORLD and colophon are registered trademarks
of Penguin Random House LLC.

Originally published in hardcover in the United States by
One World, an imprint of Random House, a division of
Penguin Random House LLC, in 2021.

LIBRARY OF CONGRESS CATALOGING-IN-PUBLICATION DATA
Names: Geller, Danielle, author.
Title: Dog flowers : a memoir / Danielle Geller.
Description: New York : One World, [2020].
Identifiers: LCCN 2020006990 (print) | LCCN 2020006991 (ebook) |
ISBN 9781984820419 (trade paper) | ISBN 9781984820402 (ebook)
Subjects: LCSH: Geller, Danielle. | Navajo Indians—Biography. |
LCGFT: Autobiographies.
Classification: LCC E99.N3 G357 2020 (print) | LCC E99.N3 (ebook)
DDC 979.1004/97260092 [B]—dc23
LC record available at https://lccn.loc.gov/2020006990
LC ebook record available at https://lccn.loc.gov/2020006991

Printed in the United States of America on acid-free paper

oneworldlit.com
randomhousebooks.com

1st Printing

Design by Fritz Metsch

For my sisters,
the little Tweets

CONTENTS

Dog Flowers

Creator

⟿⟶✦⟵⟿

MY MOTHER SPENT the last six months of her life homeless, sleeping in a park in Lake Worth, Florida. We had not spoken to each other at all in that time. But when the hospital called to tell me she was dying, I booked a flight from Boston and arrived in Florida the next morning, too late. She would not wake the two days I sat by her side.

My mother's on-again, off-again lover, Dale, met me at the hospital and told me he was holding on to her things, that I could go through them and take whatever I wanted. In Dale's closet, I found my mother's life packed into eight suitcases, which, by the very nature of their design and state of disrepair, told the passing of time. Most were filled with clothes she had picked up at thrift stores, and that was where they would return. But in the oldest—an eighties, soft-shelled leather case with wide straps and massive buckles— I found her diaries, her photos, and the letters she kept. I found a few undeveloped disposable cameras. I found a green corduroy purse filled with dried sage bundled into smudge sticks. I found the bandanas she wore on the days she skipped washing her long black hair. I found two crooked potholders she had crocheted. I found sterling-silver-and-turquoise jewelry I set aside for my sister, Eileen, who was hitching rides on semis and freight trains across the West; she wouldn't make it to the hospital in time.

I gathered the pieces of my mother's life and packed them into the newest suitcase, a navy blue carry-on, to bring home with me.

TITLE: Laureen "Tweety" Lee holds her daughter's hand behind their apartment in South Florida.

DATE: 1987 July 28

TYPE OF RESOURCE: color negatives

DESCRIPTION: My mother wears a lace-like white blouse and black short-shorts. Beside her, I look like a happy monkey-child. I am one year old. We smile for my father, who takes the photograph, which I later digitally develop from a negative strip I found in a soft paper envelope labeled "Birthday Negatives, July 28, 1987." The plastic negatives are degrading, or perhaps the photographs were never processed correctly in the first place. The resulting photographs appear gritty and washed out.

I

the way her dreams must have felt
back then,
wide and open,
 so much space to be filled.

—LAURA TOHE, "Sometimes She Dreams"

and boy it just burns me up

MY MOTHER LEFT the Navajo reservation almost as soon as she could. At nineteen, she moved to the city, as many do, to continue her education. In a brown and water-stained copy of an incomplete job application, I found evidence of these early years: From April 4, 1983, until July 1, 1984, she took classes on cultural awareness, health education, and leadership at the "Albuquerque Job Corps Center." ("It was the best," a woman who attended the school in the late eighties wrote in a recent Google review. "I will always remember the good times I had.") For work experience, my mother found part-time jobs in retail at Kirtland Air Force Base; as a file clerk at the "Albuquerque Rehab. Med. Center"; and as a typist at the "New Mexico State Labor Com.," a position she held for only a month.

In August, my mother moved to Prescott, Arizona, and began working as a waitress at the "Palace Hotel Restaurant," where my parents met. My father told me they met at the Hotel St. Michael, which was not true, but my father always loved the sound of his own name.

My father worked for his brother's computer company as a traveling technician. Those were his glittering days: He charged expensive rental cars to disposable credit cards and drove back and forth across the country. He gave the keys to his cars and hotel rooms to the homeless and traveling people he met. He dropped acid in the desert and once, he claimed, met a man entirely surrounded by a golden aura—Jesus Christ himself.

The way my father told their story, I always believed my parents fell in love quickly. That after those early smoke-filled nights, she left with him when he returned to Florida, where I was born in the summer of 1986. But the application I found was dated March 27, 1985, a few months after she quit her job in Prescott and moved back to New Mexico. The reason given: "Looking for Another type of job."

When I asked my father how my mother got to Florida, he said she called him months after they first met. "I could come see you," she said.

WHEN I CALLED Eileen to tell her our mother was dying, I wasn't sure what words to use. I repeated the doctor's words: Sick. Heart attack. Nonresponsive. Very, very sick.

She asked, from a distance, what I meant.

Eileen and I were not good sisters to each other. We never held each other, and we didn't end conversations with love. But in that moment, I would have given anything to take her in my arms, to give her some small comfort. "Her heart doesn't work anymore," I told her. "She's not going to get better."

"*What?*" My sister's voice edged on anger, an anger I had always feared.

"She's dying," I said, simply, and then listened as her anger dropped into heavy, wracking sobs. I couldn't take my words back, and I couldn't think of anything else to say. All I could do was listen to her cry until she finally decided to hang up.

She called me a few hours later. Her voice sounded like smoke rising, faint and curling. She was high. She asked if I planned to go down to Florida.

I had been sitting in front of my computer with flights mapped out, but I hadn't been able to convince myself to buy a ticket. I wasn't sure I wanted to go.

"Someone has to be with her," Eileen said. She was somewhere in Montana, and she said she would try to buy a bus ticket, but she worried she wouldn't make it to Florida in time.

The walls of my room were painted cornflower blue.

"I'll go," I promised.

"You can't go down there alone," she said, but we both knew I would. "I'm sorry, Danielle," she added, beginning to cry again. "I'm sorry."

A FEW MONTHS after my mother moved to South Florida, she was pregnant with me. My father claimed she could get pregnant off a toilet seat. My father's mother convinced her to keep the baby, and she offered them a two-bedroom apartment in a building she owned on Nokomis Avenue, a chalk-white dirt road.

Our neighbors were inconstant. My grandmother's tenants were as poor as our neighborhood, and no one seemed to stay for long. She liked to tell the story of one of her tenants who dragged all his furniture, even the refrigerator, onto the lawn in the middle of the day. She couldn't get a reason out of him—he talked nonsense, raving about who knew what, so she called an ambulance. Later she found out his rotting teeth were the cause of his madness, but she found the story funny and laughed each time she told it.

I was too young to remember most of our time in that apartment, but in my mother's things I find a soft paper envelope labeled with her neat script: "Birthday Negatives, July 28, 1987." When the pictures were taken, I had just turned a year old. In some of the photographs, I wear a white jumper; in others, only a diaper. Over one shoulder I carry my favorite pink blanket, whose corner will rough and wear from the constant rub of a finger soothed by its exposed stitch. My mother and my father and my grandmother, Evelyn, are all here.

The way my father tells those early years, my mother was the one who hit *him*. Angry-drunk, she whipped him with the cord of an alarm clock, and then she called the cops. My mother and the neighbors and I stood in our gravel driveway and watched the police chase my father down the road, around the block. The dust settled soft and white.

The way my father tells it, my mother was wrong and the police were wrong and my memories were wrong, because I did not remember the violence the way he wanted me to. I remember my father's shadow in the doorway in the moments before he threw my mother to the floor. The way she curled up under the kitchen table and stayed there, sobbing, even after he was gone. She told me to get rid of his beer. I pulled the chair over to the sink and dutifully poured each can down the drain.

My mother stayed for years after that fight, after many fights, but I remember one of her early leavings. She took my sister and me to the women's shelter at the Salvation Army. The light was all cream and yellow. We caught head lice from the shelter's temporary beds. My grandmother convinced my mother to go back to my father, her son, the way I imagine she always did. Once home, my mother washed our long hair with the special shampoos and picked the nits off our scalps with a comb, but my father, impatient, went to the store and bought a new hair buzzer. I watched him lift the buzzer from its polystyrene cradle. I cried as he cut off all my hair.

FLORIDA IS UNCHANGED and true to memory: fulgid sunlight and flat horizons, broken only by palm trees and scrubby pines. The parking lot at the JFK Medical Center sprawls confusingly, and I circle it twice. After I park, I follow a couple into the building, but as I step onto the sidewalk, a small bush rustles, and a curly-tailed lizard lands on the ground in front of me. I jump back, both startled and embarrassed. I caught lizards as a kid—even wore them like earrings, their small mouths clamped to my earlobes, their thin bodies wiggling against my neck—but this place, this lizard and I, have become strangers. I watch him for a breathless moment: his mouth open, his sides heaving. Then he darts across my path and disappears into another small shrub.

I enter the lobby through a pair of tinted glass doors and approach the officer at the front desk. He positions me in front of a camera and prints my badge on a sticky label, then directs me to an elevator down the hall. Inside the elevator, I inspect the photo on the badge: a grainy shadow you might call me.

I follow his directions out the elevator and down the hall to the critical care unit, quiet and cold. The curtain in front of my mother's room is open. Standing beside her bed, a nurse delicately washes her face.

I waver at the threshold, and when the nurse glances in my direction, she startles, as if I were a lizard landing on her path. "Who are you?" she asks.

"I'm her daughter," I say.

The nurse frowns and shakes her head. "We were told she didn't have any family. Nobody's been here to see her."

Her words land sharp and heavy on my heart. I glance at my mother's face, wrinkled and sun worn. Who did they imagine my mother to be? Another homeless woman, unloved and forgotten? Slowly, I walk toward her and rest my hands on the rail of her bed. "I came as soon as I could," I say—in her defense, and mine.

I DON'T REMEMBER when my mother left. I only remember that one day she was gone. And after she left, my sister and I stayed in the apartment on Nokomis with our father for less than a year.

In school, I was a happy student. Each day, I left my kindergarten class during the language arts period to read with the first graders. I had a crush on a blond-haired boy named Todd. During the designated nap hour, I snuck into the play area and tried to convince my friends to join me, until the teacher moved my little yellow rug to the spot in front of her desk.

At home, I was different. Quiet and small as a mouse. My father drank constantly with the neighbors and with his girlfriends, who rotated in and out the door.

My father often drank to blackout. One night, I watched my sister, still in a diaper, suck on a bottle of mustard like it was a bottle of milk. His body slumped behind her on the couch. Those nights, the windows of our apartment were like black holes devouring all light. My mind was full of the scary stories my father and my uncle told, sitting in rickety lawn chairs under porchlight: stories about ghosts and werewolves and gremlins, like the ones on TV.

My grandmother worked evenings waitressing at the Scotch 'n Sirloin, but she wrote her number on my dinosaur notepad, purple and shaped like a brontosaurus, and taped it to our fridge. Night after night, I called her at work and begged her to come get me. After work, she would pick me up and take me home, but she always left Eileen with our father because, she said, *I* was the one who was scared.

A few months after my mother left, a red-haired woman moved in with her two pale-haired children, a boy and a girl. She cooked terrible food, like ground beef and green beans mixed into dry mashed potatoes, and she tried to make me eat it by calling it "Native American food." I couldn't remember my mother cooking anything like that. My mother made us macaroni and cheese and Hamburger Helper, straight out of the box. My father's girlfriend forced food down my throat, and when I puked it back onto my plate, she yelled at me and sent me to the room we now shared with her two kids.

The four of us slept on mattresses on the floor. The boy and his sister shared one, and my sister and I shared the other, but after the lights went out, they crept under our blankets and peeled our nightgowns up and over our heads and slid their hands down. Years later, I heard my grandmother telling someone, I can't remember who, they had been abused by their dad.

My mother came home only once, when the red-haired woman was at work. I was home alone from school and watching TV on the couch with my tuxedo cat, Teddy, curled heavy on my chest. My father met her at the door. They tiptoed across the living room like cartoon burglars, and my mother giggled, "Don't tell anyone we're here, Danielly." The bedroom door clicked down the hall.

When my father's girlfriend came home, she asked, "Where's your dad?"

I was a small, contained thing: a girl on the couch. I told her I didn't know.

She walked down the hall, and then everyone started yelling. My mother, clutching a T-shirt over her bare breasts, ran out the door. I jumped off the couch and followed her into the driveway; I watched her jerk the car into reverse and disappear down the road.

In a dream that felt like that day, I followed Teddy into the empty lot across the street. The sky was loud and gray. The palmettos rattled in the wind. I sat at a wooden school desk with a white kite tied to one leg. The wind tossed the kite higher and higher, and then my father appeared with a pair of scissors and, with one snip, let it go.

A few days later, as I pedaled my bike up and down our sidewalk, my father's girlfriend complained about my mother to the woman next door. I heard her say, "She's a filthy little liar." And as I turned my bike and glanced up at her face, I realized she was staring directly at me.

When Teddy got hit by a car some weeks later, he dragged his broken body home—his two back legs struck useless and limp. He pulled himself around the apartment for a couple of days, and then he disappeared. My father's girlfriend explained that this was what cats did—they crawled off somewhere to die alone.

The sun was shining through the bedroom window when her son pulled me into his bed. His sister was jealous, standing over us. "Please don't tell," I begged. "You're next." But she ran out of the room to find my dad.

I ran after her, but she had already told.

My father grabbed me by the shoulders and leaned into my face and said, "Don't ever let a boy touch you like that again."

I can't remember what he did to the boy.

Near the end of kindergarten, my grandmother showed up at our apartment with a police officer. He brought me into the back bedroom and closed the door. He tucked a stuffed animal into my hands and kneeled down and asked, "Do you feel safe here?"

I was silent and nervously pulled at the stuffed animal's fur.

"Do you want to leave here with your grandmother?" he asked.

I said yes.

After the police officer left the room, my father's girlfriend appeared beside me and grabbed hold of my arm and hissed, "How could you do this to your dad?"

Guilt crawled down my throat and into my gut and sunk its fangs deep, but I didn't know how to undo what I had done.

On May 3, 1991, when I was five and my sister was three, the courts granted our grandmother full custody of my sister and me. My father surrendered his parental rights on the informal condition that if he could be sober for a year, we would be allowed to live with him again. My mother didn't even get that much—there was no consideration for her future custody.

IN HER HOSPITAL bed, my mother's foot moves in a small, unending circle: still seizing, the nurse explains. I cup her foot in my hand and press my fingers against the soles of her feet, hard with calluses from the work boots she wore.

The nurse watches me. I can feel her eyes. But when I look up, they are more gentle than critical. "Is anyone else coming to be with you?" she asks.

I shake my head no.

"No one?" she asks.

"Her husband died last year," I say. "And my sister can't make it down."

She nods slowly as she works. She has started a collection of my mother's blood on a metal tray. "I'll let the doctor know you're here," she says.

After the nurse leaves, I retreat to a chair in the far corner of the room to watch my mother from a distance. I can't shake the feeling there is something expected of me. Some thing I am supposed to do; some word I am supposed to say. My sister has asked me to give her a kiss, but the thought unnerves me.

When the doctor arrives, she is surprised to see me. Surprised I made it to Florida so fast. She pulls a chair across the room to sit beside me in the white light of the window. "I hope I made it clear how serious her condition is," she begins.

"You did," I say. I try to hold eye contact with the doctor but find myself looking everywhere else: her legs, crossed one over the other; her hands, clasped over one knee; her hair, twisted into braids.

The doctor offers me details she avoided over the phone: My mother came to the hospital after a seizure, and while she was awaiting evaluation, her heart attacked. My mother had tried to stop drinking, but she quit cold turkey, and the withdrawal was too much of a shock. "*DTs,*" my sister would announce later, by abbreviation alone. "I knew it."

My mother's death was preventable. If she had sought care, of course, her death could have been forestalled. She was only forty-nine.

"If we had known how sick she was," the doctor says quietly, "we wouldn't have revived her."

My eyes shift to the array of machines that are keeping my mother's heart beating, her lungs breathing, and then my eyes drop to the floor. "Is there a reason to keep these machines on?" I ask.

"Everything we are doing," she says, a long sigh, "is futile."

Futile. The word sticks in my lungs. I exhale heavily and try not to cry. I tell the doctor I am ready to let her go, and she tells me she will send a woman from hospice care to speak with me later that day.

After the doctor leaves, I slide my chair closer to the bed and take her hand, small and cold. Her eyes are swollen, her hair a tangle on the pillow. The sound of my mother's mechanical breath fills the room—a forced and dry rush of air.

AFTER OUR ADOPTION was finalized, my sister and I moved in with our grandmother and her partner, Don, who she met in a restaurant's kitchen, where he was a chef. Don was a sun-brown old man who wore golf polos and plaid pants stuffed with loose change, and he jingled everywhere he walked. He wore a full set of dentures but dyed his hair jet black and claimed his potbelly was not

fat but a watermelon, grown from a seed he swallowed years before. He cooked us dinner every night. He read the Sunday funnies
to me every weekend, with me curled up in his lap.

Don was always Don and never grandpa because our grandmother decided she would never marry him. "He'd be too controlling," she told me more than once. "He was that way with his
wives. If I married him, he'd suddenly think he could tell me what
to do."

Still, they had been together as long as I had been alive, and after
our adoption, they moved into a new trailer, a brown-and-tan
double-wide, so my sister and I could have our own rooms. We
lived in a trailer park called Meadowbrook, a ten-minute drive down
Okeechobee Boulevard from Westgate, where our father still lived.
There were no meadows or brooks in Meadowbrook—only a
makeshift putting green and a sludgy canal full of shopping carts
and soft-shelled turtles. And when it rained hard enough, walking
catfish migrated from the canal to the puddles that spawned along
the edge of the road.

Our closest neighbors were boys: two Justins, two Ryans, a
Shawn, a Josh, and a Pitt. We played dinosaurs, and cowboys and
Indians. We climbed trees and caught snakes and lizards, whose
tails broke off in our hands. If I held an anole next to my ear, it
would clamp down and dangle there like an earring—my grandmother's old clip-on earrings hurt more than they did. The boys let
the lizards bite their tongues.

One winter, a pair of tall, gray birds visited our trailer park. You
could hear them calling to each other as they flew past, day after
day. The boys, Eileen, and I learned to run after their voices, to
chase them from a distance until they chose to land. Once, we
found a father and his young daughter feeding the birds tuna fish
out of a can, but the father told us to get out of his driveway when
we ventured too close. One of the boys' uncles gave us a name for
the birds: sandhill cranes. He loaned us a book, and we crowded
around its illustrations and descriptions. Our cranes wintered in

Florida but migrated north to raise their chicks in the northern United States and Canada each spring. They mated for life. The cranes, stilted and gray with crowns of red, were the most strange and beautiful things I had ever seen.

Eileen sometimes kissed the boys. Grandma called her boy crazy, like our mother—always more like our mother than me.

I did not kiss the boys when they tried to kiss me. Once, while I played a videogame in one of the boys' rooms, he leaned close to me and whispered, "I could rape you right now if I wanted to." A group of them tried to catch me—to block me in with their bodies—but I was small and fast. They herded me in circles, and I ran myself into a fever, tears and sweat draining down my face. When I finally reached the sanctuary of my porch, they stood stupidly in the yard until Grandma chased them away.

I spent less time with the boys and more time with Don. In the evenings, after school, I sat with him while he cleaned the fish he'd caught: catfish and young sharks, and flounder when he was lucky. We listened to a radio station that played pop hits from the eighties—songs by Cyndi Lauper and Eurythmics and Madonna—which was better than the oldies station Grandma listened to. After dinner, we took nightly walks around the whole trailer park. During the rainy season, we rescued the walking catfish in white buckets and carried them back to the canal. But our main project was the garden, a small, square patch beside the shed. I helped him weed and water the garden and the flower beds that cut around the trailer. We composted our kitchen scraps in a big black bin and mixed the rich soil into the earth every spring. One of my favorite photographs from our childhood is a picture of my sister and me, framed by the garden: I hold the gardening hose proudly over my head. My shorts are stained with water, and Eileen stands beside me in tears.

One year, for Father's Day, we bought Don three rosebushes to plant beside the porch. We hid them in Eileen's bedroom closet and told her to keep them a secret, but as soon as he got home, she raced over to him and exclaimed, "Don! We got you roses!"

My sister and I each wanted Don for ourselves. His love and his time and his care were finite, and our lives had not taught us to share. Eileen learned how to smile from him—the way he hugged his lips together over his teeth. When we went camping at Sebastian Inlet State Park, Don would take us fishing separately—motoring one of us out in his small orange boat while the other stayed at camp with Grandma. He taught us how to bait shrimp and cast a line and wait out the first inquisitive nibbles to hook a fish. I loved fishing with Don: the bob of the boat on the choppy inlet; his calm and solid presence; the joy and laughter when I, at last, reeled in a fish, even if it was an inglorious sea robin, to be cast back into the sea.

When I was nine, Don got sick. Cancer, in his liver. Grandma took care of him for as long as she could. Their bed became his sickbed, and Grandma asked my father to take care of my sister and me for a while.

Our father and his new girlfriend, Fran, lived in an old, dark house in Westgate. The four of us slept on mattresses in the living room, because the two bedrooms served as a workshop and storage. The workshop was lined with tables, strewn with the innards of broken electronics—televisions, microwaves, and computers—that my father reconstructed and sold at the flea market. He let me help tighten screws and connecting wires when the spaces were too narrow and his hands too big. The other bedroom was packed with clothing and toys and glassware that Fran salvaged from the trash.

When Don was sick, we didn't visit him at home, and we didn't visit him in hospice when he was finally transferred there. We spent our time at school and at our father's, running wild in the overgrown lot behind their house. We caught giant orange grasshoppers and created terrariums for them by stuffing grass and twigs inside two-liter soda bottles. We played with a neighborhood cat, whose kittens lived inside the engine of a derelict car. Grandma brought us a picture of Don, smiling behind an oxygen mask.

One afternoon, as we sat under the canopy of the field's only tree and stroked the cat's sleek back, a yellow bird landed on the ground in front of us. Before Eileen or I had time to react, the cat pounced. I screamed, and the cat turned excited eyes toward me; the bird fluttered its wings in her mouth. I lunged at the cat, but she darted across the field, and I chased her to the edge of the space that crawled beneath our house. I kneeled down and stared into the dark, but I couldn't force myself to follow. Instead, I ran inside to find Fran, who did not chase the cat but instead stroked my hair and wiped my tears as I wailed about the cat and the bird under the house. "Why did it do that?" I demanded.

"It's what cats do," she said. Only, I didn't mean the cat. I couldn't understand why the bird had flown so close to danger.

Later, I ventured back into the field, to the patch of ground beneath the tree. I found its feathers in the weeds and collected them in a small metal tin. Years after, I would find the tin, open it, and recognize the barring and shape of the bird's feathers, still soft and yellow. It was a budgie—most likely, someone's pet that had escaped and, seeing a familiar human shape, come to me for help.

WHEN THE HOSPICE worker arrives, she leads me down the hall to a dark room decorated with stiff floral loveseats. A crocheted blanket is draped over one, and empty cans and wrappers are scattered across the coffee table. Some families camp out here, the hospice worker explains. She sweeps the blanket over the back of the loveseat, and we sit at a diagonal, though she leans forward to close the distance between us.

"Do you know anything about hospice care?" she asks.

"My grandpa was in hospice," I say, remembering Don, though I was too young and too far removed to understand what that meant.

"Good," she says, smiling. "Our program is connected to this hospital, so we won't need to move your mother far. But the doctor has informed me that we can't move her quite yet."

I frown. "Why not?"

"It's the blood pump," she says, and she sits up, her back rigid. "If we remove it now, her blood would spurt everywhere." She mimes the word "spurt" with her hands, her fingers splattering imaginary blood across the walls.

I close my eyes to the room and ask when they think it *can* be removed.

"We're waiting to hear," she says with a shrug.

"My flight leaves tomorrow," I say, cracking the knuckles of my fingers one by one. "I'm starting a new job, and I can't really stay longer."

The woman tilts her head, surprised, but says in her gentlest voice, "We will do everything we can to take care of your mother."

It's not my mother, I want to tell her. It's just her body. I have not been able to find my mother in that room.

I'M NOT SURE where our mother lived when we were at Meadowbrook. She spent years bouncing between her friends' and boyfriends' houses, and we weren't allowed to visit her at home because our grandmother didn't trust her boyfriends alone with us girls. Our visits were supervised and controlled. We visited her at work, sometimes—eating quick meals during her lunch break, or catching her at the end of a shift—but usually, we saw her on birthdays and holidays: Mother's Day, Easter, Christmas, and our favorite, Halloween.

My sister and I had birthdays two weeks apart, which meant that we usually celebrated them together. One year, my mother took us to see *The Lion King*. Afterward, we ordered lunch at McDonald's and ate pressed together in the front seat of her car. She noticed me staring at the dream catcher that dangled from her rearview mirror, its twin feathers fluttering gently in the breeze. "They're sacred," she told me. "Only Native Americans are allowed to have eagle feathers."

One Halloween, my mother and her new boyfriend, Tony, took us trick-or-treating around our trailer park. They both dressed up like clowns. Tony tried to convince us there was an alligator snapping turtle hiding in a storm drain, just like the boys in our neighborhood always would; he made us laugh. One of our neighbors gave out cans of soda instead of candy—I picked orange, and Eileen picked grape.*

Another Halloween, she took us to a haunted house. Disembodied hands reached through the walls to grab at our hair. Beneath our feet, in backlit boxes, snakes coiled into knots. At the end of the haunted house, a man in a gorilla costume started chasing us, and our mother squealed in delight. But Eileen was scared. Our mother flirted with the man in the gorilla costume while my sister cried. For years after, Eileen couldn't even walk past a haunted house at a carnival.

One Easter, my sister and I decorated eggs with our grandmother: We traced hearts and flowers on the shells with white wax before dunking the eggs in cups of dye. Little testaments of our love. We waited and waited for our mother to arrive. When my grandmother finally reached my mother on the phone, her voice was scalding. "You're really disappointing these girls."

My mother showed up late, like always.†

I learned very young that my mother was someone not to be trusted—that she would break my heart if I let her. But for Eileen, our mother was the solution to a nameless unhappiness. "I want to live with Mommy," Eileen would say unceasingly. And, always, "You don't love me."

"You *can't* live with your mother," our grandmother would respond. She sighed it. She cried it. She yelled it. There was always yelling in our home.

Eileen couldn't understand why, but I did. Our mother was an alcoholic. Our father was an alcoholic. Our grandmother was an alcoholic, seventeen years sober. "You're an alcoholic," Grandma

---

* October 31, 1995. ". . . they enjoyed it just as much as we both did."

† April 16, 1995. Easter. "Spent my afternoon with my girls! 2½ hours!"

would tell me, even when I was very young. "You just haven't had your first drink."

What I did not understand, or could not understand, was why my mother drank. I could not have known the depth of her loss: her brother, her mother, her father, us girls.

WHEN I PULL into the lot of the rental-car return at the airport, I am struck with the sudden, overwhelming thought that I'm not ready to go back to Boston yet. I circle the lot once, twice, and chew on the rough skin edging my thumbnail. All I can think of is the ocean. All I want to do is throw myself into the sea, rock with the waves, stare at the sun-filled sky, and watch floaters and seagulls vie for attention against the great, engulfing blue. All I want is to fall asleep with the smell of salt in my hair, to wake up in a new bed every day, to leave this place and all places far behind me.

A shuttle bus drops me off at the terminal, and I wheel my mother's suitcase to the baggage-check counter. Even though it could fit in the overhead compartment, it is too heavy for me to lift over my head. But when I approach the counter, the thought that they might open the suitcase or that it might get lost on a connecting flight sends me into a panic, and I dissolve into tears in front of the two men standing there. "These are my mom's things," I say, and when I think that this is it—her entire life in one suitcase—I cry even harder. I tell them my mother died—is dying—is gone, or leaving—and beg them not to open her suitcase. I don't want anything to get lost.

One of the baggage guys walks around the counter to pick up her suitcase. He places it on the scale, and then he tapes a bright purple fragile sticker over the zipper. He carries the bag to the conveyor and seems to keep his back to me.

The other man looks at me, waiting, and shakes his head. "There's nothing anyone can say that will make this feel better, and nothing but time can heal your pain."

I nod and wipe the tears off my cheeks, my hands on my jeans. "Thanks," I say and add, of course, "I'm sorry."

ACCORDING TO MY mother's diary, Grandma didn't tell her we were leaving the state until a week before we planned to be gone.*

Don died in May. His funeral was held at the Catholic church where Eileen and I attended school. My teacher, Sister Pauline, escorted me from class to the service, though I had to beg to leave school early to attend the viewing and burial in Boynton Beach. One of Don's sons and his wife agreed to chaperone me.

We arrived at the memorial home after Grandma, who was crying when we walked through the door. She rushed over to me and grabbed my hand and pulled me over to the casket, where Don lay. She started talking about a pillow, red and shaped like a heart, that she had bought for my sister and me and tucked inside his casket. Before everyone arrived, the pillow had fallen out of the casket and onto the floor. "It's a sign," she said, through tears. "We always said, whoever went first, we would send the other a sign that we had made it to the other side."

I stared at the pillow, nestled back in the casket, and wondered if it was a different kind of sign. A sign that my sister and I did not hold the place in Don's heart that he held in ours.

The evidence wouldn't support my fear. Before Don died, he bought my grandmother a new car—a teal Ford Escort—and two life insurance policies, one for my sister and one for me. When we were old enough to attend college, he said, we could cash them out. The life insurance policies weren't big—worth a couple thousand dollars each—but, with his sons' permission, he left everything he had to my grandmother and us.

Months later, Grandma decided we would leave Florida and

---

* September 21, 1996. "Danielle & Eileen stopped by w/ Grandma to tell me they are living to Penn State!"

move to Pennsylvania to live with her daughter, our aunt Ella. Grandma didn't want to raise us girls alone. But she warned me not to tell anyone we were leaving, for reasons I still don't understand. My father was in jail, and my mother had no power to stop her. According to the state, we were my grandmother's children.

In September, my aunt and uncle arrived in Florida to help us pack everything we could into our uncle's van.

As they worked, I lingered near the flower beds at the edge of our porch. I noticed a vine creeping across the ground that I had never noticed before. I kneeled down and found a watermelon the size of an egg hidden under the roses. The seed from one of Don's watermelons must have taken root in the compost we spread that spring. I fought the urge to pocket the little watermelon, to bring it with me—to hold something of Don's close until the end.

I have no memory of our last visit with my mother and Tony— only the short note in her diary marking the day.* And then a week later, we were off to Pennsylvania. We left Don's roses on his grave.

WHEN I LAND in Boston, I catch a cab back to my apartment in Dorchester. I told the hospice worker that I would be available after five, and I don't want to risk my phone's spotty reception on the T. There aren't any messages waiting for me. But as soon as I tuck my luggage into the trunk and give the driver directions, I call the hospital to see how she is doing.

"Your mother has passed," the hospice worker tells me. "I'm so sorry for your loss."

I hang up the phone and sink down into the black leather seats and watch the tops of the city's gray buildings rush past beneath an orange-tinged sky. My mother died, and I had been somewhere up there. I never even kissed her goodbye.

---

*September 27, 1996. "Danielle & Eileen are leaving this day to Penn!"

it was my fault but also

꞊꞊꞊✦꞊꞊꞊

THE APARTMENT IS dark and empty when I make it home from the airport. I lean my mother's suitcase against the coffee table in the living room and collapse onto my roommate's vintage orange couch. My cat, Little Foot, appears in front of me with a raspy squeak and bumps her butt against my leg.

"Did you miss me?" I ask her out loud. I pull an Arby's sandwich I bought at the airport out of my bag.

Little Foot sits on her haunches and pricks my knee with her paws.

"Put your little feet down," I scold, but I rip off a small piece of roast beef and set it on the floor. She hoovers it up. Between my own bites, I feed her another piece, then another. "Arby's is *good*, huh?" I laugh.

It feels strange to laugh. Strange to sit in a room that is not connected to my mother. Stranger to think of the hospital, which feels less real than this sandwich and this cat.

"Time for bed," I say, balling the foil in my hand. She sniffs persistently at my hands, but she knows these words. She follows me upstairs, to the small room we share, and I close us in for the night. I leave my mother's suitcase in the middle of the living room, where it will remain untouched for weeks.

I FIRST MOVED to Boston in 2009. Nathan, my ex-boyfriend from my freshman year of college, had been accepted to a graduate program and needed a roommate, which seemed like the perfect op-

portunity to escape my family. We moved a few days after the new
year.

I spent the first six months jobless, burning through the money I
saved working for Barack Obama's first presidential campaign. I
played *World of Warcraft,* and survived on Pepsi and turkey and
cheese on plain bagels. I didn't leave the house. I didn't even bother
unpacking—I just climbed over my piles of cardboard boxes into
bed each night.

When my money ran out, I responded to Craigslist ads until I
found a job at a local thrift store. I lived a small life. I went to work—
first as a sales associate, then as a keyholder, and then as a salaried
employee in the supply department, sorting and pricing bales of
used and vintage clothing. Then I went home and played videogames with a rotating roster of Internet boys.

Two years later, I applied for a master's program in library and
information science. I didn't have any experience in libraries or archives, but I needed a change and, I reasoned, loved books. I
learned—or tried to learn—the standards of archival arrangement
and description, which are guided by the principle of *respect de fonds,*
or provenance: the chronology of the ownership, custody, or location of a historical object. According to archival standards, records
should be maintained in their original order, if such order exists.
But during my short life as an archival assistant in libraries and archives across Greater Boston, I often struggled with this most basic
principle. I received entire collections in disintegrating paper grocery bags. I shuffled through mountains of paper scraps and newspaper clippings that resisted meaningful arrangement or description
and, tired of labeling folders "Miscellaneous," I wanted to throw
away much of what I was told to preserve. I was, I came to believe,
a failure of an archivist.

WEEKS AFTER MY mother dies, one of my roommates moves her
suitcase from its position by the coffee table to the corner of the
living room. I know I should move it out of the common area, but

I am not sure, yet, what to do with everything inside. My sister was supposed to visit. We were supposed to go through our mother's things together.

I bump into a roommate, Marie, making coffee in the morning before work. We rarely see each other. She is working overtime at the thrift store, taking graduate classes in publishing at Emerson, and filming a movie with her boyfriend and some of his friends. And I am a ghost, an unseen presence in the house: a shutting door, a creaking floorboard, a weeping in the middle of the night.

She asks if I am heading to work, and I say yes.

"Cool," she says, her eyes smiling through her bangs. "We can ride the train together."

After breakfast, we walk two blocks to Ashmont Station. The autumn wind is cold and sharp. She asks me how things are as she burrows her face into the wool of her thick gray scarf.

"I don't know," I say, balling my fists inside the pockets of my coat.

Marie and I met the summer after my freshman year of college. Her father had just died. She transferred from Oberlin to Shippensburg, the little state school in Pennsylvania where her parents both taught English and where I, coincidentally, earned my bachelor's degree. But we didn't meet at school—we met through our boyfriends, who played a weekly D&D campaign with their group of high school friends. Marie and I weren't invited to play, but we talked a lot that summer, while a family of meerkats lived their dramatic little lives on TV. When the school year began, I introduced her to my tight circle of friends, and we stayed close for two years. But I broke our friendship. I moved to Boston to cut ties with my family and, in the process, cut ties with everyone else. After years of silence, it was difficult to begin talking again.

Inside the station, she grabs a copy of the *Metro,* and I follow her through the turnstiles and onto the subway platform. "I had a fight with my sister," I say, finally. "We haven't talked since."

"About what?"

"My mother's ashes."

In the days and weeks after my mother died, I didn't do any of the things a good daughter should do. I didn't write an obituary. I didn't arrange a funeral or memorial service. I tried to call my mother's family, but the only number I could find—the number for my aunt, my mother's sister—was a dead line. I could not afford to bury or cremate my mother, but I was told to submit a notarized letter to the county describing her situation. "Include she was homeless and an alcoholic," the caseworker said, implying it would help. The county paid for my mother's cremation, and the cremato- rium held my mother's ashes while I tried to reach my sister; I wasn't sure what she wanted to do with our mother's ashes.

She stopped responding to my calls and my texts and my Face- book messages. In the silence, I scrolled through her Facebook page, largely abandoned except for the few photos she posted over her last year traveling: She sits on a sidewalk and holds a clever card- board sign asking for money. In another, her road dog, Monster, licks her face. She holds her phone at arm's length and squints into the sun with the mountains of Arizona and New Mexico behind her. She shaves her hair into a mohawk and collects new tattoos: three thin lines on her bottom lip and three dots on her chin; the letters *D O G S* written on the backs of the fingers of her left hand; a lizard on the cartilage of an ear. The ear and the tattoo were later mangled when, drunk or high, she tried to steal a bone from the mouth of a dog with her own teeth. The dog snapped and caught her left ear; with its teeth or its paw, it tore the skin beneath her left eye. The day our mother died, Eileen posted a photo I took of our mother cleaning my kitchen in Pennsylvania, from when our mother visited to attend my college graduation. Then my sister posted nothing.

When the crematorium grew impatient with my delays, I told them I didn't want my mother's ashes. I couldn't imagine her at rest in an urn on my shelf. Boston was too cold and too dark and too far from the home my mother had made in South Florida. After a week, they offered to scatter her ashes in the ocean, to send me the GPS coordinates after it was done. I told them that sounded fine.

"You did *what*?" Eileen screamed, weeks later, when she found out. "You believed them? They're probably just going to dump her in the garbage somewhere."

"So what?" I said, hearing how cold and unflinching my own voice sounded. *It isn't her,* I wanted to say. *It isn't our mother.* But she hung up.

I tell Marie she wouldn't answer my calls. "What was I supposed to do?" I ask Marie. "I had to make the decisions by myself."

"That's unfair," Marie agrees.

We lapse into silence again. When the train pulls into the station, we claim two seats in a corner of the front car, and Marie opens the *Metro* to the crossword and scratches answers inside the little squares.

I stare through the opposite window. I am an empty vessel. The ashy walls of the tunnels and the bare branches of November's trees pour in.

"Is your sister still coming to see you?" Marie asks.

"I don't know," I say, shaking my head. "She was supposed to help me go through our mom's things. But I don't think that's going to happen anymore."

"Would you like me to help you?"

"Yes," I say, closing my eyes against tears. "I'd really appreciate that."

MARIE AND I meet in the living room a few days later. I set a bundle of the sage I found in my mother's suitcase inside an abalone shell and strike a match. I have "borrowed" a records box from work and bought a stack of acid-free manila folders. I feel prepared.

I give Marie a shoebox of my mother's photographs, and I start digging through my mother's papers. I sort through my mother's opened and unopened mail. I throw out any form letters and junk mail but keep the rest: bills from hospitals, notifications from labor agencies, and letters from her family. I am surprised—but maybe shouldn't be—that my mother kept every letter my sister or I sent: commercial and handmade cards, with notes that grew longer as I grew up. I stopped sending her letters after the eighth grade.

I find letters from my mother's family on the reservation, most of which are at least a decade old. The letters are addressed to "Tweety" or "Tweetie," the nickname my mother had, she told us, ever since she was a little girl in a yellow dress. One of my mother's cousins affectionately calls us, her daughters, "the little tweets."

Marie organizes my mother's photographs by the people in them. She tries to separate the photos of my sisters and me, but we sometimes look too much alike.

"Who's Boo-Boo-Loo?" she asks from the couch.

I would not have known if I had not read an entry from her diary earlier, one in which she describes me: Bo-Bo walking around the house saying "ma-ma." "I think that's what she called us when we were little," I say.

Marie laughs. "The envelope on these pictures just says 'BuBu-Loo.'"

I take the envelope she offers and shuffle through pictures of a little girl that *could* be any of my sisters. My mother wears a turquoise shirt. The girl has cake all over her hands; my mother, her face. I don't recognize the room—not the furniture or the photos on the walls. This must be my mother's third daughter, one of my half sisters, the one born after Eileen and I moved with our grandmother to Pennsylvania. "It's Alexandra," I say, handing the stack of photographs back.

Marie hands me another photo: an eighties-style glamour shot of a man in a cowboy hat with a thick brown mustache and sultry eyes. Another photo: a woman in a leopard-print dress, who poses suggestively on a bed surrounded by stark white walls. "What *are* these?" we laugh.

My mother lived entire lives apart from mine. I am tempted to erase the questions and unknowns from my mother's life—to simplify the arrangement—but what kind of archivist would I be?

By the end of the night, I arrange my mother's papers and photographs into a series of labeled manila folders: Diaries, Work, Medical, Correspondence, and Photographs.

I arrange my mother's diaries, which she kept in appointment books, by date. The oldest diary is from 1987, the year after I was born. It is different from the others, which are cheaper and spiral-bound. The hard cover is puffy with gilded trim, and it is titled *Adventure: The Art of Living Dangerously*. In the pages between each month, the editor, Richard Frisbie, curates stories and illustrations of world-traveling adventurers like Teddy Roosevelt, Kilton Stewart, and Naomi Uemura. There is no indication my mother read the stories—the pages are crisp, absent underlining or other marginalia—but they provide a charming, if not simple, frame. "Every day used to be an adventure in staying alive," Frisbie writes in his introduction to the book. "Although circumstances have changed over the past few thousand years, we still have the reflexes of a species used to living on the edge of danger." Frisbie writes about men and women trying to survive extremes of weather and circumstance. They battle ice and snow, shark and bear and crocodile.

In 1987, my mother describes finding me crying in my crib, my father drunk at a friend's. She describes a conversation with my grandmother, in which my mother agrees to quit her job to take care of me. She writes about my father's struggle to find and keep a job. She tallies the weeks and months of his sobriety—on April 2, she records: "3 months and 2 weeks." And then nothing. The tally ends.*

I turn the pages slowly. Read most but not all of the entries

---

* July 27, 1987. "He got mad and wanted to fight the world."

aloud. I trace my fingers over my mother's careful cursive, over the destruction that unfolds.*

I realize I have forgotten that Marie is here, a silent spectator to time before memory. I close the book and rub the pad of my finger against its hard edge, as I would my childhood blanket. "It makes me feel sorry for her," I say.

Marie nods. Her silence: an invitation to talk.

But it's late. The windows dark. "I'm tired," I say instead, sliding the diary between the neatly labeled folders inside the box. The diary's dimensions are too large for its own folder. I press the lid down over the top.

WHEN A PERSON dies, the ch'į́ʼįdii is the thing left behind, like a ghost. The ch'į́ʼįdii carries the residue of every wrong thing the person was unable to bring into balance or harmony in life. The ch'į́ʼįdii haunts a deceased person's bones and possessions, exits the body with their last breath. Contact with the ch'į́ʼįdii can cause illness, a "ghost sickness," which manifests physically and mentally through symptoms you might recognize as grief.

I am not trying to learn how to grieve my mother; I have been grieving her absence my entire life. I am ghost-sick. Possessed.

---

* August 19, 1987. In red ink: "I started drinking about noon that day and by 4:30 & 5:00 P.M. I was will on my way to a blackout. We at the time we went to a Chinese Restaurant and I sure started a fight with Mike and it got worst by the time we got home. I said things that I haven't said to Evelyn and also don't really remember but any was up at 10:30 and sure felt terrible but also knew it was my fault but also that Mike should have not hit me."

EMPLOYMENT HISTORY

IF YOU HELD MORE THAN ONE POSITION WITH THE SAME EMPLOYER, INDICATE THE TITLE OF EACH JOB, LENGTH OF TIME HELD AND GIVE A BRIEF DESCRIPTION OF DUTIES. PLEASE INCLUDE ANY VOLUNTEER WORK WHICH YOU FEEL IS RELATED TO SPECIFIC JOB INTERESTS.

NAME OF PRESENT OR LAST EMPLOYER EMPLOYER OR FIRM: **Palace Hotel Resturant**

STREET ADDRESS: **116 S. Montezuma**
CITY: **Prescott** STATE: **Arizona**

SUPERVISOR'S NAME: **Jerrie Miller**
TITLE: **Owner**

FINAL SALARY: $ **2.75** PER **hour**
NO. OF HOURS PER WEEK: **30**

TITLE OF POSITION HELD: **Waitress**

DATES: (MONTH/YEAR) FROM **10,8|-18,4|** TO **11,2|-18,4|**

REASON(S) FOR LEAVING OR WANTING TO LEAVE: **Looking for another type of job**

JOB DUTIES/RESPONSIBILITIES:
Taking orders, Serving food, Wiping off counter in which I serve food from, Clearing Tables and Just satisfying customers.

NAME OF NEXT PREVIOUS EMPLOYER: **New Mexico State Labor Com.**

STREET ADDRESS: **2348 Menaul N.E. #212**
CITY: **Albuquerque.** STATE: **NM**

SUPERVISOR'S NAME: TITLE: **Terry Baca**

FINAL SALARY: $ **—0—** PER **—0—**
NO. OF HOURS PER WEEK: **10**

TITLE OF POSITION HELD: **Clerk Typist**

DATES: (MONTH/YEAR) FROM **10,5|-18,4|** TO **10,6|-18,4|**

REASON(S) FOR LEAVING: **Working as part of my work experience.**

JOB DUTIES/RESPONSIBILITIES:
Typing, Filing copies, Working with the copier machine, Operating the adding machine, and

TITLE: Application for employment with the City of Albuquerque, New Mexico.

DATE: 1985 March 27

TYPE OF RESOURCE: job applications

DESCRIPTION: Third page of a partially completed job application from Lee's job search in Albuquerque, New Mexico, in early 1985. The document is creased and stained. In blue ink, distinct from the black ink Lee used, someone has scribbled in the blank spaces. I wonder if it might have been me, as a girl.

TITLE: "I Love My DoG"

DATE: undated

TYPE OF RESOURCE: construction paper

DESCRIPTION: Illustrated four-page booklet titled *I Love My DoG* by Lee's daughter, me. It is drawn on construction paper with black marker and crayon and bound with cellophane tape. I draw my sister and me with matching blond hair, pink shirts, and purple skirts; the girls in the book do not resemble us at all. And we never owned a DoG.

TITLE: A letter from Danielle Geller to Laureen "Tweety" Lee written on Lisa Frank paper.

DATE: undated

TYPE OF RESOURCE: personal correspondence

DESCRIPTION: I wrote a letter to my mother on one of my favorite pieces of Lisa Frank stationery, a three-by-six-inch sheet with a mottled brown horse tucked inside a cloud. A rainbow arcs off the edge of the page, and I darken the borders of the clouds with my thick black marker. I place a Lisa Frank sticker in one corner: a purple kitten reaching for a psychedelic angelfish too big for its goldfish bowl. The letter is creased in the middle from being folded inside a matching envelope, though it was never mailed. It was written when we still lived in Florida and likely hand delivered.

TITLE: Alexandra Alvarez is held in the air.

DATE: 1999 November 24

TYPE OF RESOURCE: color photographs

DESCRIPTION: Someone holds my sister Alexandra high in the air. This photograph is part of a series of photographs developed at Winn-Dixie. The envelope is labeled "Little Bit."

TITLE: Laureen "Tweety" Lee and Alexandra sit together on the floor.

DATE: 1999 November 24

TYPE OF RESOURCE: color photographs

DESCRIPTION: Alexandra—"Boo Boo" or "BuBuLoo"—leans against Lee, who is seated beside a white crib. From the other photographs in the series, I know my sister wears a shirt with the Puerto Rican flag and a pair of mock Tims. My mother balances Alexandra's Elmo hat on her head. A bottle of Bud rests on the floor. This photograph is part of a series of photographs developed at Winn-Dixie. The envelope is labeled "Little Bit."

II

But it's no good to talk of the dead. It brings them back, I have heard. From wherever they are, they hear their once-name. They see a small spot in this world for them, and some will try to wriggle their way back to it, like shimmying into old snakeskin.

—Natanya Ann Pulley, "The Way of Wounds"

A FEW DAYS after Marie and I went through my mother's things, my grandmother called to tell me my sister turned herself in, to serve a years-old warrant issued after Eileen broke probation in our small Pennsylvanian town. Grandma said she would spend at least eight months in YCP, York County Prison, and she gave me my sister's inmate number to write her letters.

When we first moved to Pennsylvania, we wrote letters to our parents because our father was in jail again—too-frequent DUIs— and, in those days of exorbitant long-distance charges, our mother rarely called. In my mother's papers, I find the letters I wrote to her. I tell her about the first time we saw snow. The single sentence makes me remember, clearly, the flurries that dissolved on the warm surface of the grocery store's parking lot and the way Grandma laughed at our overexcitement. In my letters to my mother, I tell her I miss her and complain about my sister, "the brat." I tell her about our new pet, a parakeet named Ripple, who we teach to say "pretty bird." I tell her the names of the girls at school, which all end in *i* or *y,* and complain about how hard it is to make new friends.

My mother never wrote back—or, if she did, Grandma didn't give me her letters.

My father's letters arrived in envelopes stamped with red warnings: THIS CORRESPONDENCE ORIGINATES FROM A CORRECTIONAL IN-STITUTION. Grandma bought me a scrapbook and a package of photo-mounting corners, and each time I received a letter from my father, I carefully pressed it onto a new page.

With the money we sent him, my father bought a pad of drawing paper and colored pencils, and every few weeks, he sent us a new work of art. Most of his drawings featured Garfield in striped prison regalia, with a ball and chain attached to his back paw. ("You ever heard of a pet rock?" he jokes.) Garfield plotted escape and tried to order pizzas to the jail while the guards were asleep. My father sold the letterhead to other inmates for commissary money so he could buy coffee and cigarettes. I sometimes wonder how many kids and how many girlfriends might have received letters with my father's drawings, and if they saved those letters, too.

My sister's letters arrived stamped with similar warnings. Beginning in middle school, she was sent to juvenile recovery centers, foster care, and boot camp. She spent six months in juvenile detention. This would be her second time serving at YCP.

People—friends, teachers, counselors, my own family—often asked how my sister and I turned out so differently. I used to say I didn't know.

Another likely story.

⸻✦⸻

BEFORE DON DIED, we used to visit our aunt Ella in central Pennsylvania every summer. We all piled into Don's van and followed I-95 north, and each time we crossed a state border, Eileen would ask, "Are we in Georgia yet?" We would all laugh because Georgia was the first state out of Florida and because there was nothing exciting about Georgia, but she never failed to ask. To pass the time, we played the alphabet game and the license plate game and sang the old folk songs Grandma's grandpa used to sing. We colored to the sound of Don's fishing poles rattling above our heads, and I sucked on pretzel sticks, which Grandma said would settle my stomach, riled by the motion of the van.

We stayed with our aunt in her house in Red Lion, the old cigar town where she lived with her husband and teenage son. We often stayed for weeks, and Grandma enrolled us in swimming lessons at the local high school and summer programs in a park at the top of the hill. We played with my aunt's dogs, Shadow and Rufus, in their huge backyard, and I woke up early every morning to watch the songbirds breakfasting at my aunt's feeders: finches and cardinals and chickadees, whose names I learned from the colorful chart stuck to her fridge. My aunt taught me how to sit still with a peanut between two fingers; how to wait, with quiet attention, for a blue jay or squirrel or chipmunk to accept it from my hand. Don and Grandma sometimes left us with our aunt to visit Don's family in Ohio or to travel alone. One year, they took a cruise to Alaska and brought back photographs of bears and moose and killer whales. Another year, they brought us miniature Navajo sandpaintings: I received a painting of a sun shield—"by Teresa" written in pencil on the back.

After Don died and we moved to Pennsylvania for good, we lived in one half of my aunt's duplex. Eileen and I shared a bedroom, my aunt's old sewing room, which narrowly fit a bunk bed and a small writing desk.

We joined the swimming team, and every day after school, I walked to the high school for practice. The chlorine bleached my hair gold and split it at the ends. I won second- and first-place ribbons for the fifty- and hundred-meter freestyles at local swim meets. At the championship meet at the end of the season, I swam in a solo freestyle race and as anchor for our relay team, but when I dove into the water for the solo race, I failed to tuck my chin properly and my goggles slipped down my face. My goggles dragged around my neck and I couldn't breathe, not because of the goggles but because I panicked. My feet touched the bottom of the pool, and I glanced up at my coach, Wanda, who crab-stepped along the edge and shouted encouraging words I couldn't understand. I dove forward and barely finished in last place.

Wanda met me at the end of the race and wrapped me in a towel after I climbed out of the water. I cried as she led me back to my grandmother, who asked Wanda what happened. "I think she had a panic attack," Wanda said.

In the spring, my aunt gave me free rein over the flower beds in front of our half of the house. Grandma must have asked. I scattered cosmos seeds near the porch and planted pansies and petunias along the sidewalk. For Mother's Day, Ella took me to the garden store, and we bought her a pink azalea bush, which we planted near the end of the walk. Don once told me that talking to plants helped them grow, and I spent long afternoons lying on my stomach whispering compliments to my flowers and stroking the soft faces of their petals.

That spring, my uncle George took us to see the Canada goslings at Lake Redman. He gave us cracked corn to throw into the grass. George reminded me of Don—the way he quietly puttered around his shed or in the cluttered basement below the house on the weekends, when he wasn't working at the M&M-Mars factory in Elizabethtown. I watched him from an upstairs window or a seat on the stairs, unsure of how to get close. When my cousin, my aunt's daughter, found out George had taken us to the lake, she demanded to know why he hadn't taken her kids, his own grand-kids, to the lake as well. George stopped trying to interact with us girls.

By the end of the summer, the cosmos had grown nearly as tall as me. They brought cabbage white and swallowtail butterflies to the yard.

My father was released from jail, and a few months later, he mi-grated north. He no longer had a driver's license—the courts stripped him of his permanently—but his friend Danny offered to drive him to Pennsylvania. They loaded Danny's van with anything worth selling and stopped at flea markets along the way. When their van finally pulled up in front of our aunt's house and he stepped onto the curb, Eileen and I barreled into his legs and wrapped our arms around his waist, and he squeezed us hard and tight.

Sometime in the days that followed, he convinced our grand-mother to let us live with him again. He had been sober for a year, even though most of that time had passed in jail or recovery cen-ters.

We had already been planning to move. Living with our aunt had begun to feel crowded, and I had gone with Grandma to see two apartment units, one in Red Lion and one in Yoe, an even smaller neighboring town that sat in the valley between two mon-strous hills. We would need to change schools again, but Grandma liked the apartment in Yoe because it had fewer stairs. But instead of moving with Grandma, my father took over the lease of the apartment in Yoe.

My sister and I moved in with him in the fall. The leaves of the

maple tree in our front yard were shockingly pink. The cigar factory at the end of the street made the morning air smell like the
cured tobacco my father rolled in his cigarettes. He found a job as
an electrician for a company just around the corner from our apartment; they built portable office trailers for construction sites, which
they parked in a gravel lot just up the hill.

And after my father found work, he sent for his girlfriend, Fran.

Fran had been homeless when he met her, sitting on a street corner with a sign begging for money: GOD BLESS. As I would come to
learn from the stories she told me, Fran left home when her young
marriage turned violent. She lived on the streets and slept in the
woods, or under people's houses with the snakes and the spiders.
She bathed in creeks, even in Florida, even after an alligator surfaced
directly beside her and sent her screaming and naked into the woods.

Grandma helped Fran find work washing dishes part-time at a
local fried chicken restaurant. But not long after she started working, she quit or was fired for disrupting the customers with her too-
loud laughter, the shade of her warmth. So Fran stayed home. She
cooked and she cleaned and, even though my father was supposed
to be sober, she drove him back and forth to the beer store after he
finished work. He didn't even bother stocking the fridge. He just set
the case of Natty Ice beside the couch and opened beer after beer
after beer.

My father liked to have an audience when he drank, and I was
his captive. He played Pink Floyd and Styx albums on repeat. He
complained about his boss, the government, the state, while Fran
boredly sipped on her beer or slipped into the kitchen to fix dinner.

My father told me *Grandma* was the drunk in the family. She shot
a hole in the wall with his father's rifle and threw his Christmas tree
out the living room window. He said they had to hog-tie her on the
bed until the police came.

My father told me Grandma made him wear a button-down
shirt and tie to school every day, which was why he was bullied. The
other kids ran his tie up the flagpole.

My father told me he possessed some degree of genius, and his math teacher begged him to finish high school. But my father couldn't bear the torment the other kids caused him, so he quit.

My father told me, "Ignorance is bliss."

My father told me he killed a man—looked him in the eyes and shot him in the head. But when I asked Grandma about the shooting, she rolled her eyes and sighed. "He didn't kill anybody. He just shot the guy in the leg."

My father told me he was kicked out of the marines because he refused to kill a man for his country. He said he jumped onto his commanding officer's desk and threatened him with a knife.

My father couldn't recognize his own contradictions.

My father told me he met a Shaolin priest on the beach after he left the marines. The priest invited him back to his temple. "Do you know what he said?" my father asked, and when I shook my head, he answered, "You're not ready yet."

The Shaolin priest stories were some of his favorites to tell.

My father called himself "Michael the Archangel." All heaven and earth were set against him.

My father told me that I was the only one who might come to understand him, but I was too young to cleave fact from fiction; my father's fantasies from reality. I was too young to understand what my father wanted or needed from me. All I learned was that it was best to stay quiet, to wait for some future state of readiness that I had not yet attained.

I can remember my sister sitting there with me, cross-legged on the living room floor. But Eileen was not quiet or patient, and she *hated* Fran, who had stepped into the shadow of our mother. More and more, Eileen spent time away from the apartment with the families of her friends.

WHETHER THROUGH TIME or proximity, I became more comfortable with Fran than I ever was with my mother. We spent hours together on the couch watching *Jerry Springer* and *Xena: Warrior*

Princess before my father came home from work. I remember watching *Black Beauty* with Fran, and when Ginger died, the white stripe of her muzzle barely visible from underneath the black tarp that covered her broken body, we held each other and sobbed.

Fran was the first person I told when I got my period. I was eleven, but unalarmed—my fifth-grade health class had covered the basics. But finding the blood that morning, I remembered a scene from *Dr. Quinn, Medicine Woman,* a show I'd watched with Grandma in Florida. "I'm bleeding," Dr. Quinn's daughter wailed to her mother, as if she were dying. From my spot in front of the television, I couldn't imagine what had made her so upset. There was no open wound, no blood seeping from viscera.

"Why is she crying?" I asked Grandma. "It's just blood."

"You'll know when you're older" was all she said.

I was determined to be stoic, to avoid a scene. I wouldn't cry. I waited until Fran was watching TV—bent forward, elbows propped on knees. During a commercial break, I tossed four easy words across the couch: "I got my period."

"Okay," she said, without a glance.

When my father came home that night, she asked him for money to buy me pads.

"What does she need pads for?" he barked. "Just show her how to roll up some toilet paper."

I returned from school the next day to an ambush: Grandma and Fran, sitting together at the kitchen table in tears. Fran had asked Grandma for money instead, and my carefully crafted plan unraveled. Fran jumped up from the table and wrestled me into her arms and pressed her face against my chest and sobbed, "I was the first person you told."

But Grandma's gifts of pads were irregular, and Fran told me I wasn't allowed to use her tampons, so I learned to spin toilet paper like a cocoon around the thin panty liners I scrounged from under the bathroom sink. On days when the blood flowed heaviest, I ran to the bathroom between every class, flushing and re-spinning my custom pads. It wasn't long before I bled through my underwear, and then my jeans; it wasn't long before the other girls noticed.

"Hey, Smudge," the girls started calling me between classes, in the halls, with no explanation.

When I didn't give them the reaction they were looking for— I was silent in my confusion—they sent a boy after me instead.

"You know, guys aren't really into that," he began.

"Into what?" I asked. The girls erupted into laughter around us.

"I'm sorry," he said, too guilty and embarrassed to offer an ex-planation. And then he took off running down the hall.

"Can't you afford pads?" one of the girls yelled. She had green eyes and perfectly flat-ironed hair.

I fled to the nearest bathroom and pulled down my jeans to find a rust-colored stain just under my left butt cheek. I snuck to my locker and found a sweatshirt to tie around my waist, but the dam-age had already been done. "Smudge" was a name that wouldn't wash out.

That night, after Fran listened to me cry about the girls at school, she told me about the first time she got her period: She was sitting at her desk. She was wearing her Catholic-school uniform—a plaid jumper—and a full leg cast. The blood trickled, bright red against white, straight to the floor.

FRAN AND I protected each other, I wanted to believe. I remem-ber, vividly, the night Fran stood between my father and me. She cocked her fist in the air and warned my father to leave me alone.

"I'm not hurting her," he laughed.

Fran drew her elbow back, as if she would drive her fist straight through him. "Leave her alone," she said again.

My father muttered something casual, like "All women are bitches," our gender turned against him, but he let me retreat to my room for the rest of the night.

I could not protect Fran from my father, but I could protect her from my sister and myself. When Eileen tried to pick fights with

Fran, I fought Eileen back. When Fran cooked something I didn't like for dinner, like Salisbury steak, I tried to hide my leftovers; I knew she would cry if she found them in the trash, so I smuggled them to school in a green lunch box instead. When Mother's Day arrived, I mailed my mother a card, but I bought Fran potted tulips whose yellow petals were streaked with maroon, almost like tiger lilies. We planted them beside the porch, where they could return year after year.

BUT EVEN FRAN could not always protect me from my father.

Sometime that year, I adopted a lovebird from my best friend's mother. I named him Berry because his red, green, and blue feathers reminded me of the colored berries in Cap'n Crunch.

Birds weren't meant to be stuck in a cage, my father told me. They should be free. So we left Berry's cage door open, except at night, but clipped his wings so he couldn't fly. He followed us around the apartment on the floor until my father accidentally stepped on his tail. His tail feathers popped off in a clump, and he disappeared beneath the hutch in the living room, and it took me an hour to coax him out again. Until his feathers grew back, Berry sat low and puffy and refused to turn his back to me, as if embarrassed by his bare, pink butt. My father, in his guilt, strung up a series of ropes so Berry could navigate around the apartment above our heads.

One night, my father brought home a bucket of copper wire, which I helped him strip. Using the sharp edge of a wire cutter, I peeled the plastic casing off the copper in long, thin strips. Bright-eyed, Berry fetched pieces of the thin plastic to collect in the bottom of his cage, as if building a nest. My father's eyes got darker the longer he watched Berry, the more he drank.

"If you love something, you have to let it go," he said, repeating a version of Kahlil Gibran's famous quote, though I doubt he had ever read Kahlil Gibran. "If it's yours, it will come back to you, but if it doesn't, it never was." The quote often preceded his argument that I should release Berry into the wild, that he was a hostage in our home.

I tried to tell him Berry wasn't a wild bird. That he wasn't native to Pennsylvania. That he would die.

My father wouldn't listen, never listened. He coaxed Berry onto his hand and walked him to the screen door. I begged him to stop, but he tossed my bird skyward, and Berry rode a breeze into the tree in the front yard. A robin sat on the same branch. Berry trilled and bobbed forward, but the robin flew off, alarmed or confused, and left Berry calling after it.

I wormed past my father into the yard and begged Berry to come down. He shuffled back and forth on the branch, then finally fluttered to my outstretched hand.

"See?" my father chuckled, with a delighted grin.

I cupped my hands around Berry as I walked back to our door and hugged him close to my chest. When my father continued to block the door with his body, the tears I had been holding escaped.

My father made a disgusted sound in his throat. "What are you crying about?"

"Leave her alone, Michael," I heard Fran warn from the couch.

"I'm not hurting her," he scoffed, but he let me back inside.

Once wasn't enough. Once wasn't proof I owned Berry's love. The trick had to be repeated, but on a grander scale. Another evening, he packed us into the car and made Fran drive us to the grocery store, to the edge of a parking lot that overlooked a wide-open field. When I refused to get out of the car, my father grabbed me by the arm and dragged me out. I held Berry firmly in the cage of my hands.

"Let him go," my father said.

"He already came back!"

My father shook his head. "You have to let him go."

I was trapped between my father and the sky. I opened my hands, and Berry stretched his wings. Even though his feathers were clipped, the wind caught him like a fallen leaf, and he disappeared against the sun's setting glare.

At first, there was silence, but then I heard him calling for me—his cries piercing, pleading. I ran down the hill and into a tangle of summer-browned weeds. I called his name, and he repeated his high-pitched yells as I clambered up and down the hill. I found him clinging to the inner branches of a small bush. I tucked him inside my shirt and rested my hand over the small hunch of his back.

As I walked toward the car, my father approached me cautiously.

"I hate you," I said, my voice flat. Then I crawled into the back of the car.

I gave Berry back to my friend's mother, because I knew I couldn't trust my father with him. I knew he wouldn't be safe if he stayed.

WHEN FRAN DECIDED to leave us—to leave my father, my sister, and me—she made my dad buy her a bus ticket back to Florida, where she planned to live in the woods again. That life was better than the life she had with us.

Before she left, Fran pulled me into her room and gathered me into her lap. "I'm not leaving because of you," she said.

"Please don't go," I begged, clutching the fabric of her sweatshirt.

Fran rested her head against mine and said, in a voice stained gray with tears, "You are the only daughter I ever had."

Little Bit

~~~⁂~~~

OUR MOTHER HAD a new baby, Alexandra, who was born in May the year Fran left. She mailed us a roll of pink stickers with Alexandra's chubby face printed inside a starry frame.* I pasted the stickers all over my school binders and dreamed of the little sister I would meet one day.

Whenever Eileen or I tried to ask our mother about Alexandra, she answered evasively. "She's got a lot going on in her little life," my mother would say. Eileen and I understood this to mean that Alexandra, like us, had been left.

My grandmother would tell me, years later, that our mother called to ask if she would adopt the baby after my mother and Tony split up.† She hoped her three daughters might be together. "I told her she was nuts," Grandma said, laughing. "That baby wasn't even your father's."

---

*From a page titled "Project Outline" inside an old address book: "Sending Christmas cards & pictures." Under description: "Alex & Mommy!"

†Notes on the page of December 19, 1997. "Tony got home and was upset . . . so spent his day not eating and it was also terrible becuz he cancelled our engagement to marriage which I pissed!"

because I'm not that kind of bitch

THINGS WERE WORSE after Fran left. Losing his driver's license didn't stop my father from driving, and most nights after work, he would drag me with him to the liquor store to pick up another case of beer.

One night, when we were halfway home, he pulled the car over to the side of the road and groaned, "I can't drive anymore."

I watched him get out of the car and circle around the front to open my door. He pushed me into the driver's seat. "Drive home," he said, slamming the door.

"I don't know how."

My father shifted the car into drive and sighed, "The right pedal makes you go, and the left one makes you stop."

I sank down in the seat to press the gas pedal. I could barely see over the dashboard. I pointed my toe to press the pedal down, and the car shot forward. In a panic, I slammed my left foot onto the left pedal, and the car jerked to a halt. I could feel the tremors radiating from my stomach to my limbs, and I clutched the steering wheel to keep my hands from shaking. I started crying. "I can't."

"Sure you can," he said with a smile in his voice. I knew that this wasn't an argument I could win.

We continued down the street like that, both of my feet pumping the pedals, the car rocking back and forth on its axles. When I finally dragged the car to a rest in front of our apartment, my father reached over and turned off the ignition. "See?" he said. "That wasn't so bad."

Another night, my father brought me to the Glad Crab, a local bar. The sign outside was dark yellow, with a fiddle-playing, dancing crab. We sat at one of the sticky tables at the edge of the small dance floor. When the waitress appeared, she looked at me with narrow eyes and told my father I couldn't stay past nine o'clock.

"That's fine," he said. He ordered a beer and a basket of fries.

He spent his first beer rehashing the same stories I'd heard over and over and over. He complained about his boss, who he insisted was running the company into the ground.

A band was beginning to set up.

The waitress circled our table impatiently, but my father kept waving her off.

"Let me call you a cab," she offered, but my father slammed his beer on the table and crooked his finger at me to go.

As we walked toward the door, a man in a cowboy hat, one of the men who had been setting up the stage, stepped between us. "Hey there," he said, not to my father but to me.

It took me a moment to recognize my old swimming coach's husband, Coach Grimm, who coached the high school team. I had not seen either of them since we moved.

"Let me give you a ride home," he said.

I led my father into the parking lot while Coach Grimm excused himself from his band. My father's feet dragged across the gravel.

I can't remember the ride home or what was said. I am left only with the impression of winding roads and open fields and the moon's white light shining inside the car.

Night after night, we repeated the same cycles. Night after night after night. My sister and I were captive witnesses to my father's downward spiral. He picked up the phone and called Grandma to blame her for his childhood. When she stopped answering the phone, he started calling his brothers. He hired a private investigator to try and find his first son, older than me, born during his first marriage, and on Christmas, he dialed the number of every young

Michael Something he had uncovered. "I'm not your son," these men told him, but still, my father, sobbing, tried to keep them on the line as long as he could.

I remember, once, watching my father make my sister cry and feeling like I couldn't watch her cry anymore. I tentatively slid an arm around her and hugged her close. "Don't cry," I whispered, "I love you."

Eileen cocked her head like a small bird and looked into my face. "You love me?" she asked.

"Yeah," I said. But the expectation in her dark eyes sparked a sensation between my shoulder blades, the same panicked feeling of getting caught inside a shirt.

"You said you loved me," she repeated, her voice twisting the words into a taunt.

I pulled away.

On a day when my father started drinking early, I snapped. I screamed at him so loud my sister heard me from where she was playing at the neighbor's house across the street. I don't remember what he said, or what I said, or why. I ran into my bedroom and locked the door behind me.

My father followed me down the hall. "Open the door," he laughed, shaking the doorknob.

We lived in a basement apartment. The window in my bedroom was up near the ceiling, but level with the ground outside. I pulled a chair by the window and climbed out. I had nowhere to go, but I ran farther up the hill, past the second row of apartment buildings, through a small patch of woods, and into the gravel lot behind my father's construction company. I crawled under one of the office trailers to get out of the sun. I lay there for hours and ground small wells into the dirt with the edge of a rock. I wove loose nests out of weeds. I rested my chin on my forearms and watched ants feel their way over the earth. I watched green aphids, clinging to the scrubby blades of grass. I lay there long after my tears and sweat had dried;

lay there long after my sister came calling for me—not daring to go home.

MY FATHER STARTED searching singles chat rooms for a new girl-friend. He always moved quickly in love. A few months after he met Deb, a woman with her own two sons, we moved into a three-bedroom apartment just outside the city of York. Grandma took over the lease on our old apartment in Yoe.

We had been living in the suburbs of York County all along, but before we moved to the city, neither my sister nor I had realized how segregated Pennsylvania was. In Florida, our classmates were entirely mixed, but I realized I could count the number of black and brown kids in our entire Pennsylvania school on one hand. The York city school was the complete opposite—the white kids were the minority, and my sister and I became suddenly popular. I started dating one of the more popular boys, though his popularity had been earned in part because he had failed the eighth grade and all his friends were in high school. He had been in a sports accident and had an external fixator bolted to one of his thighs. He lived in one of the apartments in our neighborhood, and at night, after dinner, he sat with me on the back steps of my apartment, his arm hooked around my shoulders. We watched the stars and taught each other the lyrics to our favorite songs: He learned the lyrics to songs by Marilyn Manson and Nine Inch Nails, and I tried—and failed—to memorize the quick lines of Busta Rhymes and Missy Elliott. Some nights, we walked down the rows of apartments to his friend's, where they smoked joints and I sat, quiet and nervous.

I was years ahead of my classmates in school—even in math, my weakest subject. I became a kind of teacher's helper, correcting the other students' work during class.

A few weeks after we all moved in, Deb and her sons moved out. Deb's oldest son was in high school. And when my father drank and picked fights with Deb, her oldest son tried to stand up to my dad. Deb's son was tall and overweight, and it seemed like my father shouldn't have been able to push him around, but he hadn't grown up with violence; he didn't *want* to fight. My father shoved him against the furniture and into the walls.

The night they left, my sister and I followed them into the driveway. Deb's sons got in the car, but before she could, my father grabbed the keys in her hand. He twisted the keys, cutting her palm, and ignored her shouts to let go.

Eileen ran at our father and wrapped herself around his arm. "Let her go," Eileen yelled, swinging from my father's arm and kicking at his legs.

My father forgot Deb. He turned around and grabbed Eileen by the throat and pinned her to the ground.

Deb ran around the front of the car and leapt into the driver's seat and sped down the road.

I stood motionless but yelled at my father to stop.

Eileen screamed and kicked and clawed at him, until my father finally let go.

No one called the cops. Not Deb, not the neighbors, not us. We walked inside and sat around the kitchen table while my father drank another beer. He finally leveled a finger at Eileen and said, "I would *never* do that to your sister."

The next morning in homeroom, I watched one of the girls in my class suck her thumb, in front of everyone, and no one said anything. I had sucked my thumb until I was in fifth grade, when the dentist convinced Grandma to make me quit. My front teeth were shifting from the constant pressure, but she didn't want me to get braces. They had caused one of her sons so much pain in decades past. I still had a small raised scar on the back of my thumb where the skin had split under the constant pressure of my bottom teeth. As I watched the girl in my class, I slid my thumb into my mouth. My tongue trembled as I hooked my forefinger over my nose and, quietly, started to cry.

My homeroom teacher noticed. She kneeled beside my desk and whispered, "What's wrong?"

I stubbornly shook my head.

She placed her hand on my arm and guided me to the counselor's office. It didn't take long for the counselor to convince me to tell her what had happened the night before. They called my sister to the nurse's office, where they found the bruises his fingers had left around her neck.

A woman from Children & Youth Services made the first visit to our apartment later that night. She interrogated our father in the living room, while my sister and I sat in the bedroom upstairs.

After she left, he walked upstairs and stared at me with his serious, sober eyes. "How could you betray me like that?"

I remembered his girlfriend asking me, years before, *How could you do that to your dad?* I wanted to tell him I didn't mean to—that I was sorry—but he walked out of my room and downstairs before I could say anything at all.

A few nights later, my father sat in front of our apartment drinking with one of our neighbors, a man in a wheelchair. They started harassing a group of young black boys. The boys ran to their older brothers, and soon there was a circle of teenagers around my father and the neighbor. I ran out the back door when I heard them shouting, and I circled around the apartment building to find my boyfriend and his little brother watching from the end of the sidewalk. "What happened?" I asked.

"Your dad called them boys 'n———,'" he said. He might have been one of the teenagers kicking my father if not for his leg.

His little brother asked me to pick him up, and so I held him in my arms as we watched the teens beat my father bloody. I caught glimpses of his body between their kicking legs. They dumped my neighbor out of his wheelchair and onto the grass. My father went to the hospital that night, and then to jail.

The next morning, Grandma took us to school to withdraw us.

We would be moving back in with her and transferring to our old school. I found my boyfriend waiting on the steps before the bell. "We're moving again," I told him. I made no move to hug him, and he made no move to hug me. We made no promises to call, or to see each other after I left. Grandma called my name, and all I could think to say was "Bye."

LIFE SHOULD HAVE been easier when we moved back in with our grandmother, but in some ways, it was harder. Anything— homework, curfews, my sister's friends—could start an argument between Grandma and my sister. "You're just like your mother," Grandma often told Eileen.

In one of Grandma's favorite stories about our mother, my parents were still living together on Nokomis Avenue. I was a baby, and while my father worked, my mother was supposed to be at home and taking care of me. But when Grandma came to visit, she found me crying alone in my crib. Half-dressed, my mother came running home from the neighbor's apartment, where she had tried to seduce one of the two Indian men who lived there. When the other man came home, he'd chased my mother out.

By "just like your mother," our grandmother meant "irresponsible" and "boy crazy" and other worse things.

Before the few months we lived with our father and Deb in York, Eileen hung out with the straight-edge kids. She drew X's on the backs of her hands and listened to punk music and dyed sections of her hair cherry red. But after York, her friend group changed. She started partying with the stoners and skipping class.

Children & Youth assigned our family a social worker. They scheduled family counseling sessions, during which our grandmother complained that Eileen constantly disobeyed. Part of the problem was that *punishing* Eileen didn't seem to work. Grandma spanked us when we were younger. I was spanked once, then never again. But my sister found corporal punishment hysterical. Our grandmother didn't have the strength to hurt her, and even after

Grandma upgraded to a switch—the long, rubbery stem of some kind of Florida palm—I remember Eileen cackling as our grandmother tried to whip her into tears. "I wish I had the strength to bend you over my knee," Grandma threatened Eileen, but even the threat made my sister laugh. As we grew older, Grandma resorted to grounding, but Eileen simply crawled out her bedroom window. And even after our uncle bolted her window shut, she climbed out of mine.

My sister was in middle school the first time they sent her to a corrective boot camp, a place called VisionQuest. According to its mission statement, VisionQuest was a youth services organization for at-risk and troubled youth that offered programs "inspired by American Indian culture." In the letters Eileen wrote to us, she described spending nights in a sweat lodge and making arts and crafts with feathers and beads.

We drove to visit her every weekend on South Mountain, a two-hour drive west. During visitation, a counselor facilitated conversations between us, and Eileen cried about how much she wanted to change. She would listen to Grandma. She wouldn't skip school.

She was better the first few weeks after she came home. Then everything went back to how it had been.

AT THE END of my eighth-grade year, our mother visited us in Pennsylvania. Grandma didn't tell us she was coming—too worried she wouldn't actually show. Our mother drove north with her boyfriend, Dale. He had family in northern Pennsylvania, and they'd planned a long road trip together.

The day our mother arrived, my sister and I walked home from the bus like normal. Our grandmother was hopping around the yard.

"What are you *doing*?" I laughed.

"It's a surprise," she said, raising a camera to her eye.

And then our mother stepped out of the apartment and onto the porch.

In the first photograph Grandma took, my mother wraps her arms around my waist, and I wrap my arms around her neck, and Eileen stands beside us with both hands over her mouth. In the second photograph, Eileen and I embrace our mother between us. Our heads rest on opposite shoulders.

In the kitchen, we crowded around our small table, and my mother brought out a box of photos of us as kids. She'd labeled each photo in her neat cursive, using our nicknames: Dani and Ling. In one picture, I stand next to my sister, who is bundled in a baby carrier; I am wearing a yellow cotton dress. "It's like the one I wore when I was a little girl," my mother giggled.

After we went through her photos, she sketched her family tree on a small sheet of notebook paper—an elaborate web of her brothers and sister; aunts and uncles; nieces and nephews. Beneath the names of her parents, she wrote the names for our blood clans. "The blood clans are inherited from our mothers," she explained. "You are born to the Tsi'naajinii, the Black-Streaked-Wood People. You understand?"

I didn't understand, but I nodded. I would keep my mother's family tree locked in my fire-safe box until the day she passed.

Our mother stayed part of two days with us. We worked on a circular jigsaw puzzle, a cherry pie with a lattice-top crust. The pieces were nearly identical, with only slight variations of red and golden brown. As I hunted pieces, my mother braided my hair and scolded me for how broken and dry it had become. "You shouldn't wash your hair every day," she complained.

"How come?"

"Becaaaaause," she laughed. "It makes it all dry!" From her bag she fetched a red-and-white bandana with little pictures of Garfield on the border and tied it over my hair. "There," she chirped, patting it against my head. "You can wear this on the days you skip washing your hair."

Later that night, our mother left with Dale to visit our uncle Marty and his girlfriend, Kerri, who had moved to Pennsylvania a few months after my dad. "We're just gonna say hi!" our mother said.*

She was gone for hours. Finally, Grandma called my uncle's house. "You're really upsetting these girls," Grandma said.

But our mother didn't come back. Eileen remembers going to my uncle's house that night, but not me. I knew better. Or rather, I had lost my stomach for nights like those.

Our mother came by the apartment in the morning to say her goodbyes. She and Dale were headed north to visit his family in Perry County. They didn't stop to see us on their return to Florida. Instead, a few weeks later, she mailed us a photograph from their trip: She stands on the side of a narrow road and offers an apple to a young, half-wild deer.

OVER OUR YEARS in high school, my sister and I drifted further and further apart. I was awkward and a little bit weird, and I didn't have many friends at school. I spent more and more time role-playing in an online fantasy world called Rhy'Din, which was scattered across member-generated chatrooms on AOL. I played a wolf, Kinia, who ruled a wolf pack called the Skeksis Wolves, and I recruited a small group of friends. Together we raised families, devised new storylines, and waged wars, fracturing and rebuilding wolf packs over years of our real lives.

Playing wolves, I met my childhood best friend, Lexi, who lived a few hours south of me. We transferred our friendship to the real world when her mother drove her to visit me, and after I got my driver's license, I would drive down to visit her. One year, I joined her family on their vacation in Ocean City; we binged every season of *Gundam Wing*, and we built a fort of blankets and pillows on the stairs to race through the Anita Blake books. We made a tradition

---

* In my mother's photographs, I find pictures of my mother and Dale, smiling on my uncle's couch. In the corner of the photo, on a coffee table: a carton of cigarettes and four cans of beer.

of missing the New Year—playing videogames through the count-down. I would drive down to visit her so we could we play our lat-est favorite, *Tales of Symphonia, Disgaea,* or *Final Fantasy Crystal Chronicles,* in her basement.

I also met my boyfriend online. He was two years older than me and lived in Idaho. We played a pair of vampires, Dove and Qat, who frequented Rhy'Din's taverns and underground places. I bought calling cards with the money I earned at my job at Hardee's, and we talked on the phone every night. When I was sixteen, I con-vinced my grandmother to let me visit him over Christmas break. The rest of my family thought she was crazy, but I flew out to stay with him and his father in Boise. He showed me around his city, and I met his mother and his older sister and his nephew and his piano teacher and believed I had found love.

Eileen was more socially adept than I was, even if the friends she had chosen were walking her down our parents' path. More than once, a police officer brought her home after curfew. One night, she and her friends tried to run from the cops for breaking curfew, but Eileen got stuck trying to climb over a tall fence when she failed to find the gate. The officer brought her home, and she hopped around the kitchen—giggling nervously to herself—while he tried to lec-ture her and our grandmother. Once she saw his car pull away, she pulled a small glass pipe out of her underwear and cackled out loud.

"I don't understand what's wrong with you," our grandmother groaned.

After she was caught drinking underage, Children and Youth placed her in foster care, with a family an hour north. The family hosted a rotating roster of kids. Once a month, my grandmother and I met her and her foster mother in a restaurant off a highway exit halfway between our home and theirs.

Eileen begged us to be allowed to come home, but it wasn't up to us. She was in foster care for almost a year.

After she came home, she pushed our grandmother onto the ground during a fight. I ran into the living room when I heard Grandma yell. As she used the couch to try to pull herself to her feet, I walked toward Eileen with clenched fists.

"What are you going to do?" Eileen laughed at me.

I swung at her once, and she swung back, and I grabbed her shirt in my hands and threw her against the wall. Eileen didn't want to fight me, not really. Our grandmother screamed that she was going to call the cops. Eileen yelled her apologies, but she was sent to a second boot camp on South Mountain.

She wrote us letters between visits and listed the growing number of push ups she could do; the growing distances she could run. Grandma and I drove to South Mountain every two weeks, though I started skipping some weekends because of work. During our visitations, she promised she would change; that she would do better.

"I love you," our grandmother said, wiping tears from her eyes. "I just need you to behave."

I wanted to believe Eileen would change—that she would keep the promises she made—but I couldn't. I couldn't understand why she chose to drink, when drinking had already cost us so much. I knew that when she returned home, she would get mixed up with the same friends, and the years we had lived we would live again and again and again.

I TRIED TO kill myself. No single event precipitated it—only the feeling that nothing would change. One night, after Lexi and my boyfriend and my sister and Grandma had all gone to bed, I swallowed all the Tylenol I could find in the cabinet, which wasn't enough, and so I swallowed a bottle of liquid vitamins, too. I didn't really understand how it worked. I sat in the bathroom and cried; my stomach tied itself in knots. When I realized I wasn't dying, I walked into my grandmother's room and gently woke her up.

"I tried to kill myself," I said.

Grandma propped herself on one elbow and squinted at me through the dark. "Do I need to take you to the hospital?"

"I don't know," I said.

"Let's go," Grandma sighed, pulling herself up out of bed. She drove me to the emergency room, where a nurse, Michael, monitored my breathing and my heart. He asked me what I had taken and how much.

"She didn't do any permanent damage," he assured my grandmother. "But keep an eye on her tonight."

I was assigned a counselor, and every other week, my grandmother picked me up from school and drove me downtown, where I talked with a white suburban woman whose life seemed very different from mine. I told her about my childhood, and when she asked me what I wanted, I told her I wanted my family to be happy; I wanted to be normal.

"What *is* normal?" she asked.

I didn't have a satisfactory answer for her. She seemed to think that *normal* didn't exist. I agreed, in theory, but also knew there was a version of normal my life could have been.

I was diagnosed with depression and anxiety, and my counselor suggested I might also have post-traumatic stress disorder. My doctor prescribed me Zoloft, then Paxil, though nothing they gave me could change the chaos at home.

WHEN MY BOYFRIEND turned eighteen, he moved in with my grandmother, my sister, and me. He proposed to me and gave me his mother's ring. He hadn't yet finished high school, but his mother agreed to let him finish his diploma online. The two of us shared a bedroom, my sister had the other, and my grandmother slept in the living room on a pull-out couch.

I found a new job at a place called Checkered Past, a vintage clothing store and piercing studio in one. During the week, I went to school, came home, ate dinner, and worked most nights from four to nine. Then I finished my homework before I passed out.

Most weekends I worked both Saturday and Sunday, sometimes opening the store by myself.

My boyfriend didn't work, and he didn't try very hard to find a job. He couldn't drive, either. He spent days playing videogames— *Warcraft III* and *EVE Online*—with his friends. He complained we didn't spend enough time together and that we never went out.

I was tired all the time. Sick all the time. I missed enough days of school to fail my senior year, but the women in the attendance office knew my sister, who missed even more days of school than I did, and when graded on a curve, I excelled.

The day Eileen was expelled she laughed, "I was in the fucking bathroom. I just didn't want to go to class."

They started shipping Eileen to a school for at risk kids. Then she punched a teacher and they tossed her in juvenile detention.

ONE NIGHT WHILE I was at work, my father stumbled into the store off the street. He had been living in Elizabethtown with Deb, who had inexplicably taken him back, but she had kicked him out again.

"Danielle," he yelled as he walked through the door. "Come say hi to your dad."

The store was empty except for my manager and me, but I rushed to meet him. "You have to leave," I said, trying to block him from walking farther into the store.

"Why?" he asked, pushing past me. "I'm not hurting anybody."

I could feel my manager's gaze heavy on my back; my throat felt tight with tears. "You can't come see me like this," I said quietly, trying not to cry.

My father stopped. He looked into my eyes, and I watched something close over his face. "Are you ashamed of me?"

"I'm not," I insisted.

"Okay," he said. He awkwardly patted my shoulder. "You know I love you, right?"

I nodded. I watched him leave. I pressed my palms against my eyes to try and dry them before facing my manager again. I can't remember what she could have said.

Later that night, the cops picked up and tossed my father into a cell for public drunkenness. After he left me, he had walked down the street to a bar and started another fight.

TWO WEEKS BEFORE my high school graduation, my uncle's girl-friend died. She passed out in the bathtub and drowned. My sister was sitting in their living room while it happened—Eileen watched the paramedics carry her out of the house. They managed to revive her, but she never woke from her coma. Her religious mother flew into town from across the country and fought with my uncle about removing her from life support.

Grandma called her death a blessing. After a lifetime of drink-ing, my uncle's girlfriend had been diagnosed with cirrhosis of the liver, a disease my grandmother called a worse kind of hell.

I didn't want to attend my graduation, but Grandma convinced me to walk. She and my boyfriend sat in the bleachers and watched me cross the stage—a white robe against a brewing thunderstorm. Neither my father nor my mother showed.

BEFORE GRADUATING, I had applied to two nearby state schools and been accepted to both, but I decided to enroll at Shippensburg University because they offered me a full-tuition scholarship, and neither my grandmother nor I had been able to save much for col-lege. Shippensburg also had the better secondary education pro-gram, and I hoped to become a high school English teacher.

My boyfriend, however, hadn't finished his online high school certificate, and instead of following me to Shippensburg, he de-cided to move back to Idaho to live with his mother and stepdad. That summer, I took a month off work to stay with him and his mother before the semester began.

His mother gave him a job in her law office, and we spent days playing *Magic: The Gathering* at her office, when he wasn't filing or answering phones. She sometimes let us borrow her car, and we drove into town for lunch or milkshakes.

One weekend, we drove into the city to meet his friends at Barber Park and float down the Boise River in an inflatable raft. The river was full of families in rafts and inner tubes; the water slow and calm. We peeled off our shoes, rolled up our jeans, and sprawled in the sun. A man floated past us with a cooler tied behind his raft, and when he cracked open a beer, we made fun of him. "That seems like a bad combination," we laughed.

My boyfriend's friends handled the oars, steering us away from the banks and overhanging trees, but partway down the river, they saw too late a lone branch that jutted out of the water. Our raft folded around the branch and flipped us all into the water. I ended up at the bottom, fighting through arms and legs toward the surface, only to bump into the raft instead of air. The current swept me into a quick, rocky section of the river.

I was frantic and hyperventilating by the time I pushed the raft off my head, but I became distracted with our shoes, which floated past. I caught my boyfriend's boots by the leather straps and my sneakers by their laces, and I tucked his friend's sandals under one arm. I collected three and a half pairs of our shoes before I realized the Budweiser man was trying to get my attention. He paddled close and yelled at me to let go of the shoes.

I didn't let go of the shoes, but I did kick myself closer to him. He didn't fight me as I piled the shoes into the bottom of his raft. I held on, and he paddled us to the far bank, where the water was shallow enough for me to stand. I thanked him and gathered the shoes back into my arms, and then I started trudging back up the river, the water heavy in my jeans. The stones on the bottom of the river bruised my feet, but I didn't think to put my shoes back on.

My boyfriend and his friends were sitting under a tree with the raft, not far from where we had fallen into the water. I dumped the shoes onto the ground and apologized that I hadn't found the fourth sandal. Rather than getting back into the water, we walked the rest of the distance to the car.

My boyfriend and I walked a few steps behind his friends. "Why didn't you come looking for me?" I finally asked.

He glanced at me and shrugged. "I knew you could swim."

My grandmother mailed me a spare pair of glasses to replace the ones I lost in the river. A bruise the size of my hand darkened on my left thigh, where I must have collided with a rock. When he went to work for his mother, I stayed behind in her condo and wrote about how I had stopped believing in love.

THE DAY I left for college, my father helped me pack my grandmother's car and mine. We didn't need the space both cars provided, but they were excited to see me off. I followed behind my grandmother's car on the highway with my hazard lights flashing, because she saw speed limits as a number to drive well under, never at or above.

The school was teeming with students. While my grandmother sat in the car in front of my dorm, my father and I shuffled my packed boxes from the car to my new room. When they realized the dorm rooms weren't air conditioned and that I had forgotten a fan, they ran to the local Kmart to buy me one, as well as a new minifridge, which they noticed many of the other students had brought. They even picked up a box of Yoo-hoo and a case of Pepsi to stock the fridge.

I could tell from the shine in my father's eyes and the quick way he bustled around that he was happy—that he was proud of me. "Maybe one day you can teach me to spell," he joked before they left.

Shippensburg University was a small rural school surrounded by cornfields and cow pastures. The Amish rode their buggies downtown. I lived in McCune Hall, the honors dorm, and became friends with a group of guys who lived on the second floor. They all played videogames, and I spent hours sitting in their rooms watching them play *Half-Life* and *World of Warcraft*. My computer was an old eMachines that couldn't run many games, so when we played *Call of Duty* over LAN, I often picked a sniper rifle and found a spot on the map to camp.

I started dating a guy, Nathan, who I met on the first day of orientation. He had made fun of me for wearing long, baggy jeans and a black sweatshirt in the August heat. His parents were hippies; he wore patched corduroys and Grateful Dead T-shirts and hemp necklaces. He played the didgeridoo. Mostly, we hung out at the dorm with our shared group of friends, but some weekends, we drove down the country roads to a park or a creek, where he collected dragonfly larvae for his freshwater aquarium and tadpoles to feed them.

Away at school, my family was easier to ignore, but my grandmother left me long voice messages, complaining that I never called, and my father sent me regular drunken emails about the future of AI and about Google, the company he believed would save the world. Nathan didn't like hearing about my family, and my new friends labeled and dismissed them as crazy. I started to learn how to twist my sorrow into a joke. I laughed when I told them about how my father had broken his leg: He was so drunk, he walked into the side of a moving dump truck. Its wheel rolled over and fractured his leg in a spiral, requiring pins and screws. His starburst scar from a spider bite was buried under new and tender pink flesh. But if I laughed, they could laugh with me. I could share a piece of myself and bury the rest.

I didn't want to go home over Christmas break, but the school closed its dorms and I was forced to vacate.

My father was living at my grandmother's again, and both he and my grandmother slept in the living room, on opposite couches, the two bedrooms still belonging to my sister and me. To me it seemed ridiculous to leave my bedroom empty, but perhaps my grandmother believed I would return home more often than I did.

Grandma said my father wasn't allowed to drink while he stayed with her, but of course he did. One of the mornings I was home, he barged into my room and shouted, "You have to help me save these sorry fucks!"

I had been asleep and sat up slowly and mumbled at him to leave me alone.

He sat down next to me on the bed and tangled his hand in my hair. "Come on, Danielle," he said. "Give me a hug."

I pushed him away and told him again to leave me alone.

"When did you become such a fucking bitch?" he muttered, walking out.

Later that day, we sat around the kitchen table, and Grandma tried to feed him cold chicken salad. "Eat something and go to bed," she insisted.

My father stubbornly shook his head. "You're the reason I drink," he told her. "You taught me how. It's your responsibility."

"Shut up, Michael," she groaned.

"You don't know what it was like," he told me.

I laughed, and he shoved his plate across the table at me; stood up; stormed out of the house.

That night, I drove my sister to see a friend across town. Eileen was old enough to apply for her learner's permit, but too scared to drive. She had enough friends to hitch rides around town. In the car, my sister couldn't stop fidgeting—toggling between stations on the radio, digging through my CDs, bouncing and kneeling and turning around and around in her seat. She told me about all the new drugs she had tried—about candy flipping: tripping on both ecstasy and LSD. She liked to try and get a rise out of me. If I told her "That's dumb" or "That's dangerous," she would counter, "You should try it," and laugh. I stayed silent and gritted my teeth.

After I dropped Eileen off, I called Nathan and cried. He offered to let me stay with him at his parents' for the rest of winter break. They lived an hour north in an old farmhouse. He gave me Pennsylvanian directions: right at the cemetery on the hill, take the next

left, then look for the tall bushes; there are chickens in the yard. His
mother asked me to sleep downstairs on the couch, but after I heard
his father snoring, I snuck upstairs and into his bed. I woke up to the
sound of a cardinal, perched on his windowsill, gently tapping at his
own reflection in the glass.

I returned to school and tried to forget about my family, but that
spring, Eileen ended up in boot camp again. She mailed me letters
at school, listing the number of push-ups, sit-ups, and pull-ups she
could do. She confessed, for the first time, that she had started using
heroin. She talked about completing her GED and joining the army
once she got out. In one of the letters, she wrote, "I don't know
what's wrong with me. I don't want to fail when I leave."

Every few weekends, I drove down to South Mountain, often
without my grandmother present. Eileen cried apologies into her
hands. "I *want* to get clean," she said.

I moved home at the end of the school year and started working
at the vintage clothing store again and slowly broke up with Nathan, whose best advice about my family amounted to distancing
myself from them, which I was not prepared—nor had ever been
taught—to do. I started dating a punk I met through work, and I
met Marie, so even when I returned to school in the fall and lost
half of the friends I shared with Nathan, I found a new group of
friends to replace them with.

We had weird fruit-tasting parties and played nerdy board games.
On the weekends, we went hiking on mountain trails. I joined the
school's literary journal and we organized student readings on
campus.

In the spring, I successfully auditioned for *The Vagina Monologues,*
and I invited my sister to see my performance of "Crooked Braid,"
an optional monologue in the play, created by Eve Ensler after she
interviewed women on the Pine Ridge Indian Reservation about
domestic violence. My sister did my makeup: red lips, blue eye-
shadow.

I recited the lines in my mother's voice—slow and careful, dropping the hard consonants at the ends of my words. The monologue read like a song, like a poem, where nouns were allowed to become something else:

> *the snow was melting*
> *it was sloppy*
> *and mud*

I asked my sister after the performance how I sounded; I told her I had tried to channel our mother's accent. She said I sounded Mexican, but it was close enough.

MY MOTHER STARTED calling me more often when I left home for college. She called from her boyfriends' phones, whose numbers often changed, but I could always tell by the area code—561—that it was her. She seemed to only call when she had been drinking, which meant that she had much to say and I had very little. I laughed when she laughed, and I cried when she cried, and I always told her I loved her back, but mostly I sat quiet on the phone and absorbed every word she said. When she hung up, I recorded our conversations from memory into a Word document, so I might have something of hers to hold on to until she called again.

In those phone calls, my mother told me about how she started selling orchids on the side of the road.

She told me about her new pet turtle, Troy, who she named after a Sioux Indian she knew who didn't want to do anything but sit.

She tried to give me advice on love, in which she told me to be patient with men, because they're just men. "A really good relationship is one where you're good to each other," she said.* †

She told me she would visit for Christmas, and then for Easter,

---

* March 11, 1997. "Tony went to jail for Domestic Violence."

† March 12, 1997. "Lenore wanted me to leave him in there. I can't do that because I'm not that kind of bitch."

and then maybe over the summer. "I'll try," she promised, "but don't tell Eileen." We both knew my sister couldn't handle it when her plans inevitably fell through.

When I asked how my younger sister, Alexandra, was doing, my mother told me she was learning to speak Spanish in school. "She has a lot of things going on in her little life," my mother said. She never admitted directly that Alexandra wasn't living with her, but I could tell through her evasions that my sister was somewhere else.

On one of our calls, she asked me what was wrong, and when I said nothing, she asked, "Then why are you being so quiet?"

"I'm always quiet," I said.

"Your grandma raised you wrong in that," my mother sighed.* "But you're doing well. I can tell that. I don't know how, but I know."

I PLANNED A visit to see my mother the summer after my sophomore year ended. My sister begged to come with me.

She wanted to confront our mother—for abandoning us, she said—but when I told her it sounded like a bad idea, she yelled, "What the fuck, Danielle?" And then she laughed. "I would beat the shit out of her to make her understand."

"I just want to have a nice week with our mom," I sighed.

"That's fucked up, Danielle," she said. "I thought I had a sister, but I guess not."

Before I left for Florida, I called my mother to solidify our plans. She had found a new job, installing air-conditioning ducts in a school building, through the labor hall, which meant she couldn't afford to take time off work, but I still planned to spend a full week driving down and back.

I asked my mother if she knew how I could contact Fran. I wanted to spend a day with her—maybe take her out for lunch or dinner.

*June 3, 1997. "Nobody is ever going to tell me what I suppose to do. Not ever again and not even Lenore."

"Oh, sweetie," my mother said, "I think Franny died."

"What?" I asked, stunned.

The last time I heard from Fran, she had sent me a letter from the hospital. She had been bitten by a rabid fox while sleeping in the woods, a few months after she left Pennsylvania. She hadn't written since.

"I think she died," my mother said again.

I worked half the summer to save up enough money for my trip, and then I took a week off work and packed my clothes into a single bag. I left without Eileen, at six in the evening—partly to avoid traffic, but mostly because I preferred driving at night. I held the gas pedal low and cruised over a hundred. Each time I crossed a state line, I asked myself, "Are we in Georgia yet?" And when I finally crossed the Georgia line into Florida, the sun was just beginning to peek over the horizon. I still had eight hours to go, but by the time I arrived, my mother was nearly done with her shift at work.

These were the days before smartphones, so before I had left home, I printed MapQuest directions to the grocery store parking lot near her house, where we had agreed to meet. I pulled into one of the empty spaces at the back of the lot and sat on a parking curb to wait.

"You're so *white!*" my mother cackled when she arrived.

I glanced down at my arms, Pennsylvania pale, and said in defense, "I'm darker than everyone I know."

That just made her laugh even more, but it kept us from crying as we stepped into a hug.

We got back into our cars, and I followed her home: a square, lime-green house in Lake Worth. She was living with Ron at the time, and as soon as we walked in the door, she ran over to him and giggled, "I tol' you how big her boobs are."

That night she cooked liver and onions, and we sat on her back porch to strip the copper wire she salvaged from work. She sat in an old rocking chair with a small radio in her lap, and I sat at her feet, and I marveled that my hands remembered how to shave the plastic casing away from the wire in long, delicate coils. She folded the copper into skeins, like yarn. We didn't say much. Long after the mosquitoes chased Ron back inside, we worked together, in silence, in the fading light.

The next day, while she was at work, I ventured down roads I remembered from childhood. I followed my memories into Westgate, where I found our first apartment on Nokomis Ave. The roads were paved with new asphalt, black with crisp white lines. I followed Okeechobee Boulevard to the trailer park where my grandmother, Don, my sister, and I had lived. Where our trailer should have been, there was a heap of rubble, bordered by yellow caution tape.

I knew the rubble was mine. I recognized the brown-and-tan siding and the bubblegum-pink panel that marked the place my sister's room had been. As I crept around the debris, an anole lizard skittered along the edge of a windowpane, and I stepped back. If there were lizards, there could be snakes.

I circled the rubble and found our old Christmas tree still standing—the one I made Grandma buy when I decided I didn't want to kill a tree for Christmas. We'd gone to Home Depot to look for a pine tree we could plant after the holidays, but the only tree they had available was a star pine, which had huge, empty spaces between each of its star-shaped branches. It was the epitome of a Charlie Brown Christmas tree, and our sparse ornaments dangled pitifully, but the tree survived to be planted in the front yard. After years of hurricane seasons, it seemed, only the branches at the tippy-top of the tree remained. The rest of the tree's trunk was completely bare.

I took photos of my trailer and my tree, and then I got back into my car. I drove through the neighborhood and snapped a few more photographs of the places my friends and I had played, and then I drove back to my mother's. It felt right that my childhood home was in ruins. I was only grateful I had been able to say goodbye.

That night, my mother and I stopped at Taco Bell and both ordered steak chalupas, which she claimed reminded her of the fry bread from home. When Ron didn't come home, we sat in her living room, and she sipped can after can of beer, and she talked to me the way we talked on the phone: her talking, me listening.

After a few beers, she pulled out her wallet and flipped to the back. She had a picture of my sister and me, taken years ago. Then she pointed to a picture of a baby and said, "That's your sister."

"Alexandra," I said, in confirmation.

But she shook her head. This was a different sister. "I named her Janelle," she said, watching me through half-lidded eyes. "She was adopted by another family."

That's my *name,* I thought reflexively. They sounded too much alike. I stared at the photo and wondered, *When?* and *How?* and *Another one?* and *Why?* but said nothing aloud.

"Don't tell your sister," my mother said. "Eileen would just get mad."

I told her I wouldn't. In this I believed my mother was right: Eileen would just get mad, and no one could predict the things she would do. I would keep my mother's secret about our youngest sister until after our mother died.

The next night, my mother asked me to drive her to Sneakers, her favorite dive bar. I followed her inside to meet her friends. She bragged about how I was in college, and we played a round of bingo over a basket of fries. When I left, my mother asked if I could pick her up in a few hours, and I agreed. I went back to her house and fell asleep watching television on the living room floor. She stayed almost till closing, calling me to pick her up sometime after one.

She spent the next night at Sneakers. And the next.

In the mornings, while she was at work, I went on long drives. One morning, I drove to the coast and walked into the ocean, over the worn, round rocks that rattled soothingly in rhythm with the waves.

Another morning, Ron snuck me onto a private beach in Fort Lauderdale where he performed maintenance for a condo association. The sand was white and perfectly smooth.

Another morning, she and Ron took me with them to the casino on the Seminole reservation. She gave me twenty dollars and left me near the nickel slots. "Ron's taking me to the blackjack table," she said.

I exchanged my twenty-dollar bill for little tokens I fed into the machine. The rows of slot machines were ghostly empty, and I hopped one machine down the row each time I lost. When I ran out of money, I wandered through the casino to the gift shop, full of indigenous crafts: beadwork and buckskin and clay pottery. When my mother and Ron ran out of money, she called me and told me to meet them in the parking lot, and she laughed about "next times."

Years later, I would discover that gambling was more than a passing recreation for Ron—that gambling was an addiction that pulled him under.

The morning I drove back to Pennsylvania, I woke to find my mother already gone. Neither one of us was any good at goodbyes.

On the drive home, I stopped at South of the Border, a tourist trap on I-95 filled with statues of dinosaurs in sombreros, where we always stopped when I was a kid. I bought a bumper sticker and a pair of lawn flamingos, and then I set out on the road again.

I reached Virginia at the peak of morning rush hour traffic heading into D.C. Grandma and Don would have left the highway before we reached the city—they preferred slower but more scenic byways to traffic-clogged interstates—but I didn't think to ask my grandmother for directions before I left. I spent an hour stuck in an endless chain of pulsing brake lights, and then I pulled into a rest stop, locked my doors, and set my alarm for an hour. As I fell asleep, I found myself dreaming of a sister I could bring on a road trip like this; who could take the wheel while I napped a few hours in the passenger seat; who could pick up old license plate games and sing familiar songs with me. I dreamed of a sister who understood our mother the way I did, the good and the bad; who could laugh with me after the trip we'd had.

[Apocalypse]

~~~✴~~~

EVERY NIGHT WHEN I close my eyes, the world ends. In my dreams, the sun is dying—a cube of fading orange light. I walk into a house, where my mother lies in a canopy bed and wastes away in a white dressing gown. She hands me a clown doll with a porcelain face and tells me to take care of my sisters. I can't make myself tell her it's too late for that.

In another dream, the earth is a seed that cracks open and sprouts a world tree. The tree grows quickly and its thick canopy shrouds the world in dark. Druids tell us we must climb its branches to ascend to the next plane of existence, but the limbs are so thick that I can't even wrap my arms around them. I stand at the bottom of the tree and watch the distant flickers of light, but I cannot fathom reaching the top.

In another, I drive down a familiar road, past a church where my grandmother lives. Out the driver's-side window, I notice a black hole opening on the horizon. It pulls the world into nothing. I become aware that I am floating in a room shaped like a beehive. A single neon word in a box flashes in front of my eyes, but before I can read the word, two words branch away from it, and then four more, like the family tree my mother drew on a piece of a notepad paper. A web of lines and symbols fills my vision, and I fall through.

MY COLLEGE ROOMMATE and I walked back to our dorm one day after class, sometime during the late fall of my junior year.

A gust of wind rolled a pile of leaves toward us like a wave breaking on the shore. I thought immediately, *The world is ending again.*

I ducked behind the closest tree and curled my arms over my head. My roommate kneeled beside me and tried to coax me to my feet, but I couldn't move. I bawled.

Finally, the wind quieted. The leaves settled. She convinced me to follow her back to our room. I bundled myself in my blankets and turned my face toward the cinder block wall.

I skipped meals. I stopped being able to sleep. I fought to keep my eyes open, terrified of what waited behind my eyelids in the dark. Exhaustion nuzzled at my neck, but every time I felt myself slipping, I jolted awake.

Marie convinced me to see a counselor on campus. I hadn't been to therapy since high school, but after a few weeks of sleeplessness, I agreed to go.

I met with both a counselor and a psychiatrist, who asked me about my family's history of mental illness and substance abuse. They asked me about my childhood. They asked me about home. They diagnosed me again with depression and anxiety. The psychiatrist suggested I might also be bipolar, but I rejected that diagnosis because I didn't recognize the symptoms in my behavior; she prescribed me a different class of antidepressants from those I had taken before.

The first week I was on Effexor, I was jubilant. I skipped to class. I laughed again. But when my dose doubled the second week, the walls came tumbling down.

I was at a conference with my world literature class. Our professor, Rich, organized the trip and drove us to the hosting university, two hours north. But when I presented my paper, my voice was too loud and too fast. My hands trembled, and I couldn't sit still, and I realized something was wrong. I left the seminar room and paced back and forth in the hall until the other sessions let out.

Rich must have noticed something was wrong. He followed me into the hall to ask how I was doing. I tried to tell him that I was fine, but on the drive home, he told me to sit up front with him. My leg hopped incessantly. I clenched and unclenched my hands and willed myself not to cry. I could sense Rich watching me out of the corner of his eye.

When we got back to campus, he asked me if I would be okay.

I nodded and said, "I just need sleep."

I went back to my room and fell into bed, but when I woke up again, I was worse. I played the fastest, loudest music I could find and screamed the lyrics as tears poured down my face. I ran in tight circles across my room and, on each pass, touched the four posts of my bed.

My mother called. I answered, but I couldn't talk: My tongue jerked and stumbled in my mouth.

Alarmed, my mother called Grandma, who called me to ask what was going on.

I sobbed, "Nothing," and hung up the phone.

I called Marie, who picked me up at the dorms and drove me to the emergency room. She waited with me there for hours, and by the time I was seen, my manic episode had already worn off. The doctor prescribed me Valium to help me sleep and told me not to take my antidepressants again until I could see my psychiatrist the following week.

The next morning, my friends drove to Maryland for a birthday party, but I stayed home to sleep. After they left, I found myself sitting in my bed with a pill in my hand. The doctor told me not to take it. I knew I shouldn't take it. I clenched the pill in my hand. Someone told me to take it. *Take it, take it, take it.* So I did.

I called Nathan, my ex-boyfriend, who drove me back to the emergency room. He waited with me in the lobby. We watched people with bee stings and broken arms and stomach pains filter through the doors, and after they moved me to a small room with a bed, we waited some more. We were in the final weeks of the semester, and I told him he could leave; I knew he had work to finish. But he told me he would be happy to wait.

When the doctor finally saw me, she threw my pills away. She recommended I commit myself to the psychiatric ward until the medication was out of my system—a few days, possibly a week.

"I have three huge papers due," I said, glancing at Nathan.

He—the person I felt had dismissed my depression and anxiety when we dated; the person I expected to convince me that nothing was wrong—scratched his beard and glanced between me and the doctor. "I think you should stay."

SOMETIMES, WHEN I am at my lowest, I still pine for the week I spent in the psychiatric ward. The nurses gave us sedatives every night to help us sleep. I slept exactly eight hours every night and woke up each morning perfectly rested. The nurses oversaw a strict schedule packed with light exercise, arts and crafts, and mandatory sessions with the staff psychiatrist and counselor to manage our medications and our moods. They gave us balanced meals on neatly partitioned trays that arrived at the same time every day. They cared for us in a way I have never been able to care for myself.

My stutter lingered, but I assigned myself to the phone in the hallway anyway. Each time it rang, I ran out to answer it, and then fetched whichever resident they were calling for.

On the second day, my grandmother called me and told me not to be upset, which was how she introduced every piece of bad news.

"Why not?" I asked, my tongue stumbling into the wh and n sounds.

"Your dad's in the psych ward in Elizabethtown," she said. "He ran out on Deb and got drunk, and they sent him there instead of jail. They thought it might help."

I thanked my grandmother and hung up the phone. I tried not to let her words shake me. The uncomfortable parallels. But I couldn't help but feel that I would never escape my father—that a piece of him was lodged somewhere inside me, and I would never dig it out.

My friends visited me at the hospital. They brought me assignments from my classes and wireless notebooks to write in, but I didn't get much work done. Instead, I spent most of my hours visiting other residents on the ward. One of the men in my group counseling sessions was near retirement, but that year, he had experienced his first crippling depression after a surgery that left him unexpectedly weak and, from his perspective, useless. He only left his room when the nurses made him, so I visited him there to just sit quietly and talk. After a few days, he started joining me in the evenings in the common room, where I pieced together jigsaw puzzles and told stories that made the other residents laugh.

In my sessions with the counselor, I talked about the other residents more than I did myself. "You're not here to help them get better," my counselor finally said. "*You're* here to get well."

My father was released from Elizabethtown before I was, so he and my grandmother both visited me while I was still in the hospital. I told them the psychiatrist confirmed I had bipolar disorder, but he was curious about my father's diagnosis. My father shrugged uncomfortably. "Delusional psychosis," he said, then laughed. "But I made them think that. These doctors are so easy to trick. You just tell them what they want to hear."

My grandmother told me he was prescribed a short-term antipsychotic. The medication was meant to relieve his symptoms of psychosis, but they were not a long-term cure.

On one of my final nights in the ward, the man I had befriended noticed my stutter was fading. We were both surprised. I wasn't aware the other patients thought my stutter was a permanent fixture, or how well I could mask my own fragile state of mind.

I DON'T REMEMBER much of the year that followed. My doctor prescribed me lithium to treat my bipolar disorder and a benzodiazepine to treat my anxiety, but both my mood swings and my anxiety were worse than they had ever been.

That summer, I fell in love with a man I met online and drove four hours to meet him in a hotel room in the middle of New York State. A few weeks later, after the semester ended, I moved into his apartment. I was convinced I was going to marry him, but I struggled to find a job in New York. I spent all day playing videogames and then, in the middle of the night, driving back and forth between New York and Pennsylvania, alternating the time I spent with my boyfriend and my college friends. I stopped at the same Sunoco to refuel each night and fantasized about fucking the gas station attendant, Bob, in the bathroom around back.

That same summer, I fell in love with another man that I met playing videogames. He lived in Alaska but was turning thirty and talked about how he had always planned to leave his home state before then. I convinced him to move to Pennsylvania, and I helped him find an apartment near my college so we could see each other during the school year. He sold everything he couldn't pack into his little car, then started the weeklong drive across Canada. I stopped loving him before he was halfway across the country. I offered him a single hug in the grocery store parking lot the night he arrived; he smelled harsh, like Irish Spring. I introduced him to my friends only once. They all thought I was crazy. *Boy crazy, just like your mother,* Grandma would have said.

I fell in love with one of my best friends and then, just as quickly, fell in love with another. When I realized Marie was torn between our friends and me, I gave her an out. "They need you more than I do," I said.

I believed I could handle everything myself.

I limped through my last year of college. I stopped taking both the lithium and my antianxiety medication cold turkey, which made me sick and irritable. For over a week, I couldn't get off the couch. "You're withdrawing," one of my friends told me when I couldn't bridge the connection myself.

I started cycling through mania and depression again.

Manic, I got into my car and drove long, inexplicable distances. To Ohio, in the snow, to visit another man I met online. To my sister's new apartment, even though I knew she wasn't home.

My sister had started stripping as soon as she turned eighteen. Her new profession turned our grandmother's face red, but Eileen made more money than any of us, and she moved into a series of her own apartments in York, then in Littlestown. She briefly tried selling Kirby vacuum cleaners with one of her boyfriends, but nothing compared to the fast and easy money she could make dancing.

I drove an hour to my sister's apartment and picked up a rock in the parking lot. I imagined smashing the glass pane of her front door and breaking in. I imagined rooting through her fridge; sitting down on her couch; watching daytime TV. Everything I did or planned to do made so little sense. I threw the rock over a fence and drove home.

To drown my mania, I bought bottles of cheap vodka and cranberry juice and started drinking until I passed out.

DESPITE EVERYTHING, I graduated on time. My mother planned to stay two weeks in Pennsylvania with my sister and me.* When I called Eileen to tell her how long our mother would be staying, we both had to laugh. "What do you do with a mother?" we asked.

Our mother arrived a week before my commencement ceremony, while I was still finishing final exams. My grandmother didn't understand how busy I would be. Instead of visiting me at college, my mother spent most of her first week at my grandmother's, eating meals and watching TV with my grandmother and my father, who was sleeping on her couch again.

Between classes and exams, I drove home—an hour and a half each way—to see them. One night at dinner, I watched my parents

---

* Bible study notebook. March 23, 2008. "I called Eileen to wish her Happy Easter and about money but she doesn't have any so I just told her not to worry about it and I talk to Dani and she said she send me some. I just said not to tell Grandma so she won't worry."

lovingly tease each other over a dish of instant potatoes. I remember thinking, *They could have been good parents. There could have been so much love.*

After dinner, our mother gave my sister and me gifts she had promised. I received one of our grandmother's blankets, a Pendleton blanket dyed orange, yellow, and forest green. Eileen received a polyester shawl, fringed and periwinkle blue. I could tell, and my mother could tell, that Eileen was disappointed.

"I was a Yei' Bi' Chei dancer," our mother said. The shawl was one she wore to dance in a healing ceremony.

But even after our mother explained the shawl's significance, Eileen believed my gift was better. She told me so later that night. My blanket *looked* more Indian than her shawl; it told a better story on its own than either of us could tell.

I DROVE MY mother and my sister back to Littlestown, where my mother planned to stay with my sister for a few days. That night, we took our mother to the strip club where Eileen worked. She paraded us around the club and told the bartender to add our drinks to her tab. Then she led us past the main stage, dimly lit and Kelly green, to a circular booth along the far wall. Three men sat around the table, but it was hard to make out their faces in the dark.

"This is my mom and my sister," Eileen yelled over the music.

"Can we buy dances from them, too?" one of the men asked.

"Don't be gross," she laughed.

Another looked at me and grinned. "I see who got the ass in the family."

"And the belly to go with it," I said.

"We could work that off, babe," he said, shifting his hips under the table.

My mother playfully slapped his arm and cackled. "Ooh, you're bad!"

Eileen ferried us to an empty table. She was working that night, and my mother and I were left on our own. I finished my first drink, and then another, and another. I lost track of how many my mother put on our tab. When Eileen found us grinding against each other to the music, she grabbed my arm and pulled me against a wall.

"You guys need to stop," she warned me.

"Why?" I laughed. "We're just having fun."

"You're embarrassing me," she said.

My mind flashed back to the last time I had visited Eileen at work—a few weeks earlier, with a couple of new friends from college. At the end of the night, the DJ invited amateurs onstage for the last song, and I climbed up to dance. We weren't allowed to remove our clothing, but I peeled my leopard-print socks off my feet and flung them into the air. My sister recovered one from under a table, but not the other. The next morning, hungover, I clawed my way to the bathroom, and when I pulled down my pants, crumpled bills fell onto the floor. I landed heavily on the seat and collected them with wondering fingers: four single dollar bills. I couldn't remember what had happened the night before.

"Why do I have money in my pants?" I laughed as I walked back into my sister's living room.

"You don't remember?" she asked.

Eileen's hand was now tight around my arm, and her eyes were sober. Serious. Her eyes were my eyes, reflected back at me.

"Fine," I mumbled. "We'll leave."

At the bar, I found my mother sitting in a man's lap. She begged me to let her stay; he offered to take her home. But I grabbed her by the arm and cajoled her out the door.

A DAY AFTER I left, my sister's boyfriend punched through one of the small glass panes on her front door to break into her apartment. My grandmother dropped my father off to fix the broken glass. My sister called to tell me our parents had *sex*. Her voice loud, incredulous.

I laughed. "Of course they did."

"They can't get back together!" my sister yelled.

I promised her they wouldn't. But our parents were both drunk at one in the afternoon and she couldn't handle them by herself, so I agreed to drive back down.

As soon as I walked in, Eileen pulled me into her bathroom and shut the door. She sat on the edge of the tub and clutched a bottle of beer. "They're out there talking crazy," she said, "about how there's no God, but everything is connected."

There was a hole in her bathroom floor, near one of the feet of her old clawfoot tub. I stared through it at the yellowed tile in her downstairs neighbor's kitchen and made a noise like *mm* or *yeah*.

"That's what I think, too," she said, "and I don't know if what they're saying is true, or if they're just crazy, and I'm crazy for thinking the same things."

"We're all crazy," I said. I meant to sound reassuring. I opened the door and led her back into the living room to our parents. Our mother teetered on our father's leg with one arm wrapped around his neck.

"Your dad's not the man he used to be," she cackled, gleeful. "He got *fat*, and he couldn't even keep it up!"

My father looked at my mother like a love-dumb dog.

"That's gross," Eileen complained. "Don't talk about that."

I sat in my sister's computer chair in the corner of the room and listened to my father's professions of love; my mother's laughter; my sister's groans. I was surprised Eileen hadn't seen this coming. When she described stripping to me, she made it sound like providing therapy with a different wardrobe: She spent hours listening to men lament their marriages, their career failures, their loneliness. But Eileen couldn't see our father from the same distance.

After he finally passed out, I offered to take my mother back to school with me so we could separate them for a while.

In the car, my mother asked me if I was a lesbian.

I laughed. "What makes you think that?"

She looked out the window and smiled. "Nothing. Just something your grandma said."

"I've fooled around with a couple of girls," I admitted. "But I think women want more than I can give."

My mother laughed. "Yes! They're so needy!" She told me she had dated a woman, a trucker, a couple of years back.

The farms and the fields and the woods rolled past.

"When your grandma dies, someone's going to have to take-care of your dad," my mother finally said.

I stayed quiet. I knew she was right. Or rather, I was raised to believe that was true. I always assumed that person would be me.

"I'll do it," she said, surprising me. "You just send him to me, and I'll take care of him."

Neither of us knew then, or could possibly believe, that she would be the first to go.

IN HER DIARIES, my mother writes very little about that visit. She ticks off the places the bus stops: Orlando, Savannah, and Washington, D.C. She stays "At Eileen House." She attends church with my grandmother. She fills her diary with vague pronouns. "It bother me. Stay up half the nite." My father bothered her? My grandmother? Something my sister or I did? I can never know.

"Mom's proud!" She writes the day I graduate.

"What a sad day," the day before she leaves. Sunday. Mother's Day. "We waited for Mike to come home so we have a family dinner but he never show up. Upset grandma & Eileen and me." She leaves me out of the upset; I don't remember this final meal, and it is possible I wasn't there.

When she returns home, she gets trashed with a man named Glen. She plays bingo at Sneakers and goes to karaoke. She hooks up with and runs away from a man named Vinnie, "becuz of booze." Her grandmother dies. She gets into a fight with a woman over Glen and Vinnie, and the woman calls my mother a hooker, but, she writes, "I just didn't listen & went to bed." She moves back in with Dale.

* * *

THAT SUMMER AFTER graduation, I volunteered for Barack Obama's first presidential campaign. I received volunteer housing at a bed-and-breakfast a few blocks away from my grandmother's new apartment in Red Lion, in a subsidized senior living community at the old Opera House. My father helped me move out of my college apartment. I tried to sort through and discard what I could, but he just shoveled everything into giant trash bags to be stored in my grandmother's closet. I kept what I needed—some clothes, my music, some jewelry—in the back seat of my car.

I worked ten- and twelve- and fourteen-hour days for the campaign. We spent four hours every evening phone banking, and during the day we drove around the city to register voters and canvass neighborhoods. I walked the cracked sidewalks of downtown York and the baking parking lots of shopping malls. I walked the fairgrounds in the rain. I walked the hilly routes of my childhood neighborhood and the empty streets of Etters, where the clean white stacks of the nuclear power plant across the river eerily loomed over the town. At noon the siren in the main square howled, loud and louder, filling the whole blue sky with sound. I walked a neighborhood in the city on the Fourth of July. I was surrounded by people standing on the sidewalks, on the lawns, on their porches, cheering, proud. I could feel the heat from the city's fireworks on my face. My skin turned as dark as my mother's.

That summer, my sister found out she was pregnant. I tried to convince her to terminate the pregnancy if she couldn't get clean. But she fell in love with the baby that wasn't yet a baby. We fell in love. Between canvassing, I started giving my sister rides to and from doctor appointments. On Sundays, when the rest of the organizers in the office took the morning off, I woke up at five A.M. to drive my father to the flea market where he rented a little gray shed to upsell the junk he found at yard sales. I brought stacks of voter registration forms to hand out. I got into weekly debates with another vendor, a man who rented a shed a few lots down from my father's. He had a Confederate flag tattooed on his arm.

No one in central Pennsylvania knew how to talk about Obama. Every night, I cried tired tears over the phone numbers I was supposed to call. One night, a man threatened to lynch Obama if he became president. Another night, a mother of a school friend warned me to never call her about that Muslim again. Another night, a woman claimed Obama killed babies, and I broke down on the phone. I told her about how my sister was pregnant and a heroin addict; how if my sister couldn't take care of that baby, no one could. "I love that baby already," I told her, "but that isn't enough." I stunned the woman into silence, but it was impossible to know what effect my words had. When I hung up the phone, I noticed my friend staring at me. "Damn" was all she said.

Every night, I drank while entering data and listening to the daily conference call.

At the end of the summer, I was offered a paid position with the campaign. My boss, who knew about my family's issues, asked me if I needed to transfer to a different office, to get away from them, but I told him that wasn't necessary; I could focus on work.

A few days later, I slipped away from the campaign and drove south on the highway until I found a hotel with a steakhouse and a pool. I floated in the water for an hour, then ordered a steak and a baked potato for dinner. I called an ex-boyfriend and asked him to meet me there for a quick hookup, and after, asked him to leave again. The next morning, bundled in the crisp white sheets, I ate the cold leftovers with my hands.

Back on the campaign, I started falling asleep on the drive to my volunteer housing at night, and then I started falling asleep on the drive to work in the mornings. I didn't know how to balance my energy or my time.

One night after work, Nathan drove down to catch a few drinks with me at a bar. He told me he had been accepted into a graduate program in Boston, but the cost of living was high, and he needed a roommate. It seemed like the perfect opportunity to go. He asked me if I might be interested in moving with him. I admitted I didn't have a plan for what I would be doing after the election—I hadn't even started looking for the next job—but I had a difficult time imagining the next few years in Pennsylvania. I told him yes.

On Election Day, I spent hours hiding under my desk until one of the other volunteers found me. A man was looking for me, she said. The vendor from the flea market and his wife had turned up at the office; they had decided to vote for Obama, but they weren't sure if they were registered to vote, or where to go. I looked up their precinct and printed directions to their polling location.

I found out neither my father nor my sister had registered or planned to vote.

After the election, I spent a few short weeks at my grandmother's. At first I slept on her couch. If I slept too late, she ran the vacuum in the living room, clattered the dishes in the sink, and complained loudly to herself that she was alone, lonely, that everyone hated her. I set up my computer on her kitchen table and played the new *World of Warcraft* expansion later and later into the night, until I was heading to bed as she was waking up, and then I started sleeping in her bedroom after she got out of bed each morning.

Nathan and I took one quick trip to Boston in November to look at apartments. We stayed with his cousin, who lived in South Boston, and scouted listings close to the university. We signed a lease for an apartment in Allston, a popular student neighborhood.

Before we left, his cousin offered to take us out to lunch at a nearby diner he loved.

While we were waiting for the train, Nathan and his cousin carried on a conversation—about school, or work, or family, I didn't hear. The city was bigger and louder than I imagined; the people close and in constant motion. I stared at the far wall of the subway and retreated into my own thoughts.

"Helloooo," his cousin laughed, waving his hand in front of my eyes.

I blinked my staring eyes and closed my open mouth.

Nathan touched the back of my head and said warmly, "She's a space cadet."

After the New Year, we rented a Budget truck. I packed a few suitcases of clothes and blankets, and a few boxes of books and notebooks from school. I packed a shoebox of photographs, and another box of photo albums. I packed a file box of my records and letters, and a small firesafe of my most important documents, like my Certificate of Indian Birth. I packed a box of my childhood toys and another of VHS tapes, which my sister and I had divided in half. My grandmother didn't have enough space to store my things. I had no childhood home to return to. So I brought everything I valued with me.

[Pretty Little Thing]

⁓⁓✦⁓⁓

DALE, MY MOTHER's on-again, off-again lover, calls me often after she dies. He cries so long and so deeply that I imagine his mustache dewy and glistening with tears. He misses my mother. He asks me to send him photographs of her and of them together. He tells me that I am his daughter now.

Each time he calls, I ask him if he has heard anything from my mother's family. If he has found the address book with their phone numbers or mailing addresses. Each time he tells me he will keep looking.

I want to stop answering his phone calls. I am tired of pretending to listen to him. But in many ways, he feels like the only tether between my mother, her family, and me.

DALE CALLS TO tell me the woman who raised my sister Alex has asked for my name. She wants to add me on Facebook. I am ecstatic; I tell him to give it to her.

She sends me a friend request a few days later, and I give her my phone number and tell her I had been hoping to meet my sister ever since she was born. She declines a phone call and says she has only one thing to tell me: My mother didn't want Alex to know about us until she turned eighteen years old. She is only sixteen. "She only know me as her mom," she says.

I tell her I understand, though I don't. Alex grew up knowing the name of her father, but not her mother. She grew up inside a lie.

I find Alex's profile through her mother's Facebook page and send her a friend request. She accepts. I stalk all her social media profiles, finding both her Instagram account and her Tumblr page.

I share the photographs I find with Eileen.

"She has your eyes, your cheeks, your chin," Eileen says.

"I know."

"She has my crooked bottom teeth."

Almost immediately, Alex blocks me from her Facebook page. Her mother warns me not to contact my sister again, but I worry. From the things she posts on Tumblr, she seems alone; she seems depressed. She reminds me of myself at her age. I tell her mother that I believe I could be a good sister to her, that I could help her with the things she is going through.

"You don't know her," her mother says, "and she doesn't know you yet. And if you going to think like that then I really don't need that in my life. She is very love by everyone."

I stop messaging her mother. There is no arguing or persuading or communicating with a person like her.

THE LAST TIME I talked to my mother, it was November; the sky, cold; the trees, bare. She was crying. She struggled to tell me that she found Ron, her ex-husband and sometimes-boyfriend, dead; he had hung himself from the back of their bedroom door.*

I stared at the sidewalk, dotted with dirt-encrusted gum. In one moment, I considered asking my mother to come stay with me in Boston, and in the next, anger chased the thought away. My mother only ever called me when she felt guilty about the distance between us—only ever called me when she needed reassurance, for-

---

*I find no record of that day in my mother's diaries. At the beginning of November, she mentions a yard sale with Ron. On November 14, 2012: "Running out of money. Call back to unemployment to make sure everything done. Ron & I are sick. 4 beers left so Ron let me drink it." On November 21: "Moving freezer food and can goods out of house." On November 30: "Went to Police Department to get report of death for Ron."

giveness. I told her I was sorry, an apology as hollow as her love felt to me.

"It's okay, baby," she said, her voice suddenly dry. "Mommy's friends are taking good care of me."

"That's good," I said.

She told me she was back with Dale. He was grilling in their backyard. She told me they had a garden, and they were trying to grow tomatoes and corn and beans. I responded in single syllables. She told me she loved me, then hung up.

MY FIRST NIGHT at the hospital with my mother, Dale hitched a ride there. Even though he and my mother had dated intermittently for over a decade, I had only met him once before—when he and my mother took a road trip to Pennsylvania together when I was in the eighth grade. Still, I recognized him the moment he crept into my mother's room: his hunched shoulders, his thick mustache, and his graying mullet, squashed beneath a baseball cap.

"Hi, Dale," I said, standing and tightening a thin hospital blanket around my shoulders.

He didn't even look at my mother. He crossed the room and latched his skinny arms around me and mumbled apologies into my hair. For a moment, I thought he had started to rock me in his arms, as if I were a child, but then I realized I was the one carrying his weight as he swayed drunkenly on his knobby legs. I could smell the cheap beer on his skin, the cigarette smoke on his clothes.

My mother's nurse appeared in the window, her low brows and downturned mouth wordlessly asking, *Is this man bothering you? Should I ask him to leave?*

I wanted to say yes, but I shook my head no.

Dale leaned back slightly and gripped my shoulders with his hands. "You look just like your mom," he said, "such a pretty little thing."

It was and is difficult for me to understand why my mother loved

Dale—what kept her going back. His touch revolted me, and I had to pry myself out of his arms, keep my mother's bed between us, to tolerate him there. He was the last person who saw my mother alive, and for that alone I needed him.

Dale staggered to my mother's bed and slowly took one of her hands in his.

"What happened to my mom?" I asked, knowing only the pieces the hospital had given me—that my mother had had a seizure, and Dale had brought her into the ER; that she had suffered a heart attack during that hospital visit.

"She was livin' down in the park with her friend Heidi," he began, his head nodding under its own weight.

My mother had been homeless; the reality was startling. In our last conversation, my imagination populated their lives together with old and familiar props—in their garden, a radio played country music, and a case of beer warmed under a golden Florida sun. I never considered an alternative. But the image of my mother that I'd carried in my head for six months was wrong. I lost sight of everything in front of me and tried to conjure her other, actual, life— begging in the sun, sleeping on the ground, and living on beer and bologna sandwiches like the ones I helped my grandmother make at church when we packed meals for the homeless. I would draw smiley faces in mustard on the bologna slices, then flatten the smileys with a piece of white bread.

I stirred and asked him why she had been living in the park.

"Your mom was real sad after Ron died."

"I know," I said.

But I didn't, know. When my mother called to tell me about Ron, she seemed as sad as she had always been. But maybe I hadn't listened well enough. I let myself believe she was okay without me, and I let months pass without asking how she was doing or how she was holding up. And then she was gone, and there was no phone call I could make, no bus ticket I could buy, that would bring her back to me.

Dale and I stood across from each other, silent. He swayed forward and caught himself on the bedrail and made a sound that wasn't quite a laugh, wasn't quite anything. "Your mom went back and forth between us so many times . . . you know, I actually started to like the guy. But how could he? How could a man do something like that over money?"

"I don't know," I said.

He told me my mother moved in with him after Ron died, but she didn't get along with his roommate, so she left again. She lived in the park with her friend Heidi. But a few days before she died, she moved back into his house. She quit drinking, cold turkey. She was sick and refused to eat anything. She had a seizure, and then another.

"I've been through them with her before," he said, and slow tears rolled down his cheeks. "I'd just hold her tight, you know?" He scrubbed the tears away with the back of his wrist. "She drank too much," he said. "I always told her she drank too much."*

"I know," I said. But I thought, *it would have to be bad—really bad—for a man like Dale to tell you that you drank too much.*

He stopped talking. He stared down at my mother, considering, and then leaned over to give her a kiss. It was a long, slurping kiss, his lips feeling around her respirator like a catfish digging in the mud. His hand, the one still clutching the bedrail, bumped a button that sent the mechanical bed's motor whirring.

"Dale," I said over the sound of my mother's bed rising. The longer the motor ran, the more anxious I became. "Dale," I pleaded. "It's time to go."

Dale had offered me a place to stay the night and a chance to go through my mother's things, so I gave him a ride home. When we walked into his house, Dale's roommate was sitting in the living room watching *Jeopardy!*. Dale offered introductions, but his roommate hardly glanced up. His roommate's dog, though, trotted

*February 1, 2013. "I sold my DVD's so we could have beer money."

across the floor and bumped into my legs, his tail beating the leg of the wooden table that filled the front room.

"That dog loved your mom," Dale said.

I have always been nervous around dogs—I don't speak their language—but I smiled and patted the dog's head and stroked his ears.

The house smelled like cigarettes, and the tile floor was off-white, tracked with dirt. I sat down at the table and focused on the burger I had picked up on the drive and I tried not to look at all the things that collected in the corners of the room.

I couldn't understand how my mother had lived in a house like this. When my mother visited me in Pennsylvania, she cleaned my kitchen from top to bottom, scrubbing the inside of my oven and reorganizing my cabinets. She wiped down every surface; swept and mopped the floor. I'd never learned how to clean to my mother's standards—I always seemed to miss something. When I washed the dishes, I left the silverware in the bottom of the sink. When I swept, I left crumbs along the baseboards. But Dale's house might have been—must have been—cleaner when my mother still lived there.

After I finished eating, Dale showed me into the room he and my mother shared. The room was empty except for a long dresser and two twin mattresses: one bare mattress on the floor, and the other propped against the wall. He opened the closet, stacked high with suitcases. "The things hanging at the top are mine," he said, rubbing the side of his neck, "but everything else is hers. She left a couple things on top of the dresser, but I didn't touch nothin'."

I thanked him, and he wandered back into the living room.

I began with my mother's dresser. She had a few stereotypical Native American knickknacks: a dream catcher; a painted clay vase, accented with rabbit fur; a wooden chalice, carved with buffalo. It was impossible to know where she had gotten them—if she had brought them with her from the reservation, or if she had received them as gifts. Regardless, I wrapped the vase and chalice in T-shirts and set them aside.

One of the dresser drawers was full of cassette tapes, but I left all of those behind.

In Dale's closet, I found my mother's suitcases. Cross-legged on the floor, I opened her diaries for the first time. I paged through her most recent diary, digging for clues about the last few months of her life. She wrote about breaking her clavicle and being in and out of Dale's house. She snuggled up with someone she called "Jimbo." The way she wrote about the men in her life reminded me of a young girl gushing over her first loves.

I read the sentence "My things are all fill with Bed Bugs," and as soon as I did, I kicked my own bag toward the door, away from the suitcases that surrounded me. I kept reading, but I could feel them, phantom bugs, crawling down my arms and through my hair.

"How you doin'?" Dale asked, poking his head through the door.

I said I was fine and avoided his eyes. I shuffled through a stack of letters and set them aside.

He moved past me and casually flipped the mattress that had been propped against the wall onto the floor, next to his own. "You can sleep here when you're ready," he said. "This is where your mom slept."

I stared at the mattresses. Before I arrived, he had mentioned a spare room, with a spare bed. I stared at the mattress and wondered if Dale would dare try to wrestle me into the shape of my mother.

"Do you have bedbugs?" I asked suddenly, and I began to stack my mother's things—her diaries and her photographs and her letters—into the smallest suitcase, a navy-blue carry-on.

"Bedbugs?" he asked, and he chuckled quietly. "Maybe one or two. But I got a little gecko in here that keeps 'em in check."

"Actually," I said, zipping the suitcase closed, "I have a friend in West Palm I haven't seen in a long time, and she asked me to come stay with her tonight."

"Oh," he said, sounding surprised. "You sure?"

"Yeah," I said. I stood and started stacking the rest of my mother's suitcases back in his closet, one on top of another. A little lizard suddenly darted out of the closet, past my feet, but froze between Dale and me.

"There he is!" Dale yelled, and he stomped one foot toward the lizard.

I stood motionless as he tried to herd it back into the closet with his hands.

"Get back in there before the dog gets ya. He'll eat you up!"

I wanted to scream. I wanted to cry. I wanted to beat him with my fists. The lizard scurried under a pile of clothes, and I threw the last of the other suitcases into his closet, shoved it hard against the wall, and grabbed my bag and the carry-on off the floor. I carried them to my rental car, and Dale followed me outside. I closed the carry-on inside the trunk.

"Will you come back tomorrow morning before you leave?" he asked as I slipped into the driver's seat. He balanced his hand carefully on the open door.

"Of course," I said, forcing a smile.

He waved me off as I pulled out of the driveway and drove down the street. Legions of stray cats crisscrossed the road. I stopped after a couple of blocks and called a videogame friend who had offered to pay for my plane ticket and a hotel room when I first learned my mother was dying. I had been too stubborn, or maybe just felt too guilty, to accept.

I told her what had happened with Dale; I told her I felt unsafe. I asked her to find me directions to the nearest bedbug-free hotel. "*Anything,*" I begged.

She promised to call me back.

As I waited, a man rode a skateboard through a cone of street-light. A dog galloped a few feet behind him. Its leash dragged on the ground.

I worried I was taking advantage of my friend. I worried I was no better than my mother or my sister who, my grandmother claimed, used people for money and only thought of themselves.

The man and his dog appeared and disappeared farther down the road.

"I made you a reservation," my friend said when she called back. She gave me directions to a Hilton near the airport and told me to call again if I needed anything.

At the hotel, I tried to hand the concierge my credit card, but she only smiled. "It's already paid for."

As soon as I walked into the room, I shook off my clothes and left them beside the door. I walked into the bathroom and filled the tub with water as hot as I dared. When I climbed into the water, my knees and breasts broke the surface, and my skin pebbled in the air. I imagined I was back in the ocean, the sun warm on my face. I let my head sink beneath the water and squeezed my eyes shut and listened to the rush of blood in my ears, which sounded just like the ocean's waves.

I set my alarm for seven. I slept soundly and did not dream.

The next morning, I kept my word and drove back to Dale's house before the hospital opened for visitors. We sat at the table in his living room, and he cracked open a can of beer.

He told me about how my mother took care of him when he had cancer; she was there with him through the diagnosis, the sickness, and the chemotherapy.

I watched a palmetto bug crawl across the table in a shaft of morning light.

"I really loved her," Dale said with tears in his eyes. "I don't think I realized that until after she was gone."

I followed him from the house into the backyard, where his roommate was using the edge of a shovel to scratch weeds from between the patio tiles.

"He's starting the garden," Dale said, gesturing to a row of potted plants. "We got some jalapeños, and some tomatoes, and"—he laughed, nodding at a small marijuana plant—"you know what that is."

I smiled a smile that didn't reach my eyes and walked to the edge of the patio. The would-be garden was an empty patch of dirt, baking in the sun. The dog dug deep furrows in the earth.

"He tracks that dirt all over the house," Dale said, pointing at the trail of muddy paw prints that led through the back door. "Your mom used to call them 'dog flowers.'"

I looked again at the mud blooming on the ground and tried very hard to see what my mother had seen.

I MAIL DALE a small album of all the photos my mother had taken of the two of them together, and then I stop answering his calls. His number appears on my phone every few days for a couple of weeks, and then it stops.

I would still now want him with me

—⁑—

BEFORE MY NEPHEW was born, Eileen moved from her old apartment into one in Red Lion, near our grandmother and our aunt. I helped her move in before I left. We painted matching portraits of snails to hang above my nephew's crib.

Eileen still didn't drive, so while I was home, I sometimes gave her rides to and from McDonald's, where she worked most nights.

Her boyfriend, the father, moved in.

"His mom is Native," she told me one afternoon as I drove them to the grocery store.

"Athabaskan," he said, from the back seat. "A crazy Indian, like yours."

I find out, years later, that she got pregnant the night he broke into her apartment; the night she found out our mother and father had slept together on that graduation trip. Eileen was overwhelmed. She didn't love him—had already left him—but she felt alone and vulnerable. It was easy to fuck him, to forget.

I visited my sister again a few months after I moved to Boston, a few weeks after my nephew was born. Eileen had to teach me how to hold him. His socks slipped off his little feet. He had our mother's eyes and her ears and her nose.

I don't know how long my sister was clean. My grandmother told me that her boyfriend started dealing, and then that my sister started dealing, but there was no way for my grandmother or me to know. A year later, Eileen was charged with possession and tampering with physical evidence; I would find the public records on York County's website. The courts sentenced her to probation for twelve months. She started attending NA meetings and talking about God. But not long after, she started using again. She broke probation, and the courts sentenced her to confinement at YCP. She surrendered custody of her son. *She's just like your mother,* Grandma would have said; would say.

A few weeks later, Eileen sent me a letter. "I seen dad in jail," she said. She described walking back to her cell from medical, and on the way, spotting my father looking hungover and lost in his prison jumpsuit. "I was hoping I'd run into you," he said, wearing the weird, knowing smile he got when the universe aligned the way he always envisioned it should. In her handwriting, large and sharp: "It freaked me out."

But before her letter even arrived, my father called to tell me his version of the same story. When he told me he saw Eileen in jail, I assumed he had visited her, but he told me he ran into her in the hallway. He had been picked up on a drunk-and-disorderly, and spent a few days in jail.

I pried for more details, because I was confused—didn't they separate the sexes?—but my father didn't want to elaborate.

"Do you think I could come and see you in Boston for a couple of days?" he asked. His voice sounded small.

"Of course," I said, without thinking.

Instead of calling to tell me he'd bought a ticket, my father called from the bus to tell me he was already on his way.

I was supposed to meet a guy from OkCupid for a first date that night—I should have canceled, but I didn't. We met at a bar a few blocks from my apartment. I ordered a taco and a strawberry margarita.

When my date mentioned he smoked weed and relaxed with a beer every night, I panicked. "I don't really drink," I said, prodding my straw against the bottom of my margarita glass. "Alcohol makes me nervous."

"Really," he said.

It wasn't a question, but I felt compelled to elaborate. Most people don't talk about family trauma on first dates, but as my father's bus tore through the miles between Pennsylvania and Boston, the distance I had placed between my adult life and my childhood felt distressingly small.

"My parents were alcoholics," I began. I told him my mother left when I was young; that my grandmother had adopted me and my sister, but she had let us live with our father for months or years at a time.

"Maybe we should talk about something less serious," he suggested.

But once I started talking, I couldn't stop. I told him about the time my father, as a teenager in Colorado, had shot a man on a ski slope but pled criminal insanity and served his sentence in a psychiatric facility. In his twenties, in California, he'd tried to set fire to a building so the owner could collect the insurance money, but he was too drunk or too high and set himself and his truck on fire instead. Later, in his late twenties, when my sister and I were little and still living with him on Nokomis, he called the White House and threatened to kill the president if they didn't let him speak to the president on the phone. The FBI showed up at our door and hauled the three of us to the police station. They called Grandma to come fetch us girls, and when she arrived, she begged them not to press charges against my dad. "He isn't going to hurt anybody," she told them. "He's just a drunk."

Laughing, I shared these stories about my father as if they were charming anecdotes, even though my date avoided my eyes and tried to sidetrack me with questions about what I studied in school and what books I read.

After we finished our meal, he claimed he was supposed to meet his friends for pool across town. He didn't invite me to tag along.

As we were walking out, I spotted my roommate Nathan unexpectedly drinking with his cousin and his cousin's wife by the bar. I parted from my date and joined them for another round of drinks.

"How was your date?" Nathan asked.

"I don't think he's calling back," I laughed, and I quickly explained to them how the date had derailed.

They steered the conversation back to Nathan and his new girlfriend, who had been over to our apartment a handful of times.

"Don't you think she has daddy issues?" I asked. "All she kept talking about was what her father wanted her to do with her life."

"Who has daddy issues?" his cousin asked, and we laughed.

Sometime between my second drink and my third, I answered a call from a number I didn't recognize. A man on a bus told me my father would be getting off near Harvard Street.

"My dad's here," I announced, standing to leave.

Nathan looked at me, his mouth set in a frown. "Good luck," he said.

I walked outside and into the drizzling rain. From beneath the bar's awning, I watched the 57 bus pull away from the curb. A cluster of students scurried away. My father wasn't there. I realized I had forgotten to ask which bus my father was on.

I pulled the hood of my jacket over my head and started walking. I waited on the corner across from a tattoo studio where the 64 and the 66 buses stopped, but they came and left without him. I wondered if I might have already missed him, so I started walking home. I waited on my front porch for twenty minutes, constantly checking my phone, but as my buzz started to wear off, I berated myself. I knew better; I should have been sober.

The clock edged past midnight, and I jumped off my porch and started walking north, toward Harvard Square. I felt like if I just started calling his name he would hear me. I turned down Western Avenue, where the 70 and the 86 buses ran, and then I cut back toward my house. As I approached the McDonald's, I found my father sitting on the sidewalk, his feet drifting into the street, his head between his knees.

I stopped beside him and said his name.

He lifted his head and stretched his arms toward me. "Oh, Danielle," he groaned. "I got lost."

I hooked my arms under his and helped him stand. The smell of alcohol was thick on his breath.

"I knew if I just started calling your name you would come find me," he said.

"You've been drinking."

"I stopped to ask for directions," he mumbled. "If I'd—if I'd just turned left."

I walked him back to my apartment. The weight of his body was heavy on my arm.

The next morning, I tried to establish ground rules: No drinking or smoking in the house. But when I came home after work, I found him sipping from a giant McDonald's cup full of orange drink mixed with cheap vodka, as if this weren't an old trick. As if I wouldn't be able to tell he was already drunk.

I stood at the end of the couch and clenched my hands into tired fists. "What is the one thing I asked you?"

"I'm not hurting anybody," he said, beginning to roll a cigarette.

"What is the *one thing* I asked you not to do?" I repeated.

"I had a *little* to drink." He swiped a few threads of tobacco onto the floor. "I don't see what the big deal is."

"You don't respect me."

"Yes, I do," he laughed, and he smiled up at me—his dark eyes glassy and far away.

"You don't," I said, shaking my head. "I asked you not to drink, and you did it anyway. This is *my* apartment. I'm not a kid anymore."

"It's just another state of mind, Danielle." He ran the tip of his tongue along the rolling paper's adhesive and sealed it with a pinch of his tobacco-stained fingers. "Like when you were in the hospital and you had that stutter. Do you remember? Do you understand?"

I understood.

My father was stuck. His mind was an old record, the grooves scratched and collecting dirt. The needle skips backward, repeating the same notes.

"Your grandmother was a worse drunk than me," he said. "You had it easy."

"Easy?" I repeated. "I had it *easy*? You say that because you don't remember. You drink, and you blackout, and you don't remember anything. But I remember. I have to live with it every day."

My father avoided my eyes.

I wanted to make him remember—the way he treated us, the things he did, the things he said. I recited my memories—my childhood on Nokomis, the years with Fran in Yoe, and the short, terrible months in York—but the more I talked, the louder my voice became. I screamed at him, out the open windows, for the whole world to hear.

"I'm sorry, Danielle," he said, reaching for me with his hands. "Can't you forgive me?"

"I'm leaving," I said. I grabbed my keys and my wallet and ran out of the house.

I had nowhere to go. No friend I felt I could call. I walked circles through my neighborhood and brushed the leaves of vines growing on fences; avoided dogs barking in their yards. I walked until my calves burned and my head ached, and then I walked back to my apartment.

I was relieved to find him asleep—head back, mouth open—on the couch.

I went to my room and closed the door and passed out.

I woke, hours later, to his weight on the edge of my bed.

He rested his hand on my shoulder. "You're right," he said. "I don't remember."

I sat up, and he pulled me into his arms. "Please forgive me," he begged, his body shaking with tears. "Forgive me. Please."

"It's okay," I whispered, beginning to cry. "I forgive you."

The next morning I went to work, and when I came home, he was sober. We didn't talk. My father was always short-tempered and quiet when he didn't drink. We sat on the couch and watched one of his favorite films, *Alice's Restaurant,* set in a deconsecrated church-turned-home. Alice, the titular character, opens a restaurant in a nearby town. She is involved with a man named Ray but has an affair with Shelly, an artist and ex–heroin addict. In one of the final scenes, Shelly returns to the church obviously high. Ray beats him until he reveals his stash, hidden in his art supplies, and then Shelly leaves on his motorcycle and dies.

My father was a boy in the sixties and missed the antiestablishment, antiwar, countercultural movement that he idealized by a decade. Instead he grew into a punk, shaving his hair into a mohawk. He and his brothers all had motorcycles; my grandmother described them riding the bikes up and down the wooden stairs to the second floor of their apartment and parking the bikes in the living room.

He was also a heroin addict, before my sister and I were born. He contracted hepatitis B from a needle and spent half a year unable to get off my grandmother's couch. A few months into his illness, Grandma asked him to install a toilet paper holder, then found him weak and sweating on the bathroom floor. I never learned how my father stopped using heroin, but it was possible his illness was enough to scare him straight.

My father didn't stay with me long after our fight. He bought a bus ticket back to Pennsylvania, back to my grandmother's couch.

A FEW MONTHS after my sister was released, I received a call from a New York number I didn't recognize. The man on the phone told me he had bought my sister a bus ticket, arriving at three-thirty in the morning, and asked if I could pick her up.

At the time, Boston's public transit stopped running at one, but I convinced Nathan to give me a ride to South Station. He waited in the car while I ran inside.

In the center of the bus terminal, my sister sat perched on one of three gigantic suitcases. She was draped in a lime-green shawl that kept falling off her shoulders as she tried to right the suitcases that kept toppling over. I tried not to laugh.

She followed me outside, to Nathan's two-door car. Only two of her suitcases fit in his trunk.

"What do you even have in these?" I complained.

"God, just put it in the back seat!" she snapped.

On the drive home, I watched her reflection in the rearview mirror. Nathan's back seat was too small, and so she reclaimed her perch atop her suitcase—teetering back and forth each time the car took a turn. She wove an elaborate story about the man from New York, who was an opera singer she had met in a club. He had offered to let her stay with him while she and her girl-friend got clean. There was another house; his son; more names than I could remember; shenanigans with a phone. The story ended when he found out she was using again and kicked her out.

She told me she wanted to get clean. I didn't believe her, but I agreed to help.

We let her stay in the same spare room my father had stayed in a few months before, but we didn't give her a key to the apartment, because she couldn't be trusted alone.

Every day, she rode the train downtown and tried begging for money—she told people she had lost her Charlie card, or forgotten her wallet—but she came home with more spare subway tickets than cash. She tried to find work at one of the only strip clubs downtown, but she missed the audition, or wouldn't make enough money, or didn't like the club—her stories always changed. Instead, she called some of her old contacts, men with too much money, to wire her hundreds through Western Union.

One night, after I came home from work, I sat with her in the living room and listened to her rattle off a list of all the drugs she had tried. The list began with the usual suspects—heroin, ecstasy, LSD—but also included dozens of pharmaceuticals and acronyms I didn't recognize. Her eyes glowed. It felt like she was testing me— like she was trying to see how far she could push me before I snapped.

"I'm not going to sit here and listen to you glorify this," I said, finally. "You sound just like our dad."

Eileen groaned. "When are you going to realize our parents' lives weren't that bad, Danielle? You're the miserable one," she laughed. "You're not happy."

I shrugged and tried to change the subject. "Why don't you just go back to Pennsylvania and serve your time?"

"I'm not a criminal," she said, but her voice got louder. "I didn't do anything wrong."

"You did do something wrong," I said. "What about your son?"

Eileen rolled her eyes. "I'm leaving." She leapt out of the chair and paced toward the kitchen. "I'm not going to sit here and listen to you. You sound just like Grandma."

I followed her through the kitchen, upstairs, to the tiny spare room. As she texted one of her new friends, who lived a few blocks from me, to come pick her up, I surveyed the room: Her entire life—her clothes and her makeup and her photo albums and her lingerie and her sketchbooks—was scattered across the floor. I skirted around the edge of the mess and picked things up, piece by piece. I tried to find a logical place for each thing, but she dropped to her knees and used her arms to shovel pile after pile into her suit cases like a front-end loader.

"Why do you even have some of this stuff?" I asked, holding a heavy-framed photograph of her high school best friend.

"I don't know," she snapped.

Her phone rang, and she answered, "Hey, baby"—her voice suddenly sweet and small. She spun the fantasy of a girl lounging on a chaise as she fumbled with the zipper on her suitcase. She leaned heavily on the suitcase to try and squeeze it closed, but instead of groaning with the effort, she giggled a tinkling giggle for whoever was on the phone. She dragged two of her suitcases out of the room, and I picked up the last and followed. Halfway down the narrow stairs, Eileen tripped over her luggage and tumbled the rest of the way down.

I froze in place and squeezed the banister. "Are you all right?"

"What do you care?" she yelled back. Then, in that other voice, apologized to the man on the phone.

I followed her through my apartment to the street, where her friend waited in a car parked out front. I helped her load the bags into his car, and then she closed herself into his passenger seat. We didn't hug or say goodbye; she never even got off the phone.

An hour later, she called me from the bus terminal. She didn't have enough money to pay for her extra bags and wanted to know if I would pay her friend back if he swung by. She told me she could send me money later, but I knew she wouldn't. I told her no.

"Why do you always have to be such a bitch?" she asked, and then hung up.

MY FATHER SPENT the next two years bouncing back and forth between my grandmother's and his girlfriend's apartments. He spent a few short months in South Carolina, where he slept on the steps of a courthouse and on other people's porches; he claimed the cops didn't bother him in South Carolina the way they did in York. One summer, he emailed me with plans to hike the Appalachian Trail, complete with photographs of camp stoves built out of aluminum cans and tea candles. Then he told me he wanted to build a tiny house; he tried to convince my grandmother to buy him a small plot of land in West Virginia. But mostly, he sat in my grandmother's apartment and watched the few channels they got through public access.

My sister spent the next two years avoiding the warrant for her arrest. She kept a low profile on social media and rarely texted me. She spent a few months traveling with one of her girlfriends. She hopped freight trains and hitched rides with semis across the country. She slept on the street, like our dad.

When my mother called, she asked me how my father and sister were doing. I told her the few things that trickled through my grandmother to me and acted like I knew more than I did.

so I can take-care of him

───✦───

MY GRANDMOTHER CALLS to tell me my father, who had been living on her couch, is on the street again. He visited Eileen in jail, and then he returned, drunk, to my grandmother's apartment, where he ran into the building supervisor and said things he shouldn't have said. The supervisor decided his presence would no longer be tolerated in the building and kicked him out for good.

"If he just kept his mouth *shut,* he could have stayed here," Grandma says, her voice cracking.

My brain floods with the memory of their lives together in the old Opera House: my father's tobacco plant growing on the wide windowsill; his junk piled high in the corners of the room. The smell of his cigarettes and the sound of my grandmother's second-hand emphysema, a persistent, dry cough.

"Your father was a real help to me, Danielle. He cooked dinner. He did my dishes. He cleaned the apartment."

"I know," I say, chewing on my lips.

My grandmother tells me the shelters are full so near Christmas. She tells me that my nephew's father had to drive him to another county for a bed. She is worried, but all I can think is that this has happened before and will happen again, and again, and again, without change.

AFTER MY GRANDMOTHER calls, I dream that one of my teeth fractures into a thousand small pieces. I have been ignoring a bad tooth for five years. I first noticed it during the Obama campaign, when it started as a small abscess, a fluid-filled sac on my gum. Between phone calls, I lanced the abscess with the sharp edge of a fingernail. But the pain has been getting worse; the tooth is loose in its socket. At work, I press my tongue against the tooth and rock it back and forth to ease the pain and pressure in my jaw.

I finally schedule an emergency appointment with a dentist whose office is a few blocks from my apartment. The building is a converted tenement house, and I am unnerved slightly by the slanted floors and off-white walls. When the assistant leads me to the only chair, I notice a hole in the floor, like the one in my sister's old apartment, which spies on the tile of the floor below.

The dentist doesn't believe me when I tell him I have an abscessed tooth; the rot lies underneath the ceramic filling, and the tooth appears fine at first glance. But when he prods the tooth with his metal tool, he laughs in surprise and exclaims, "It's loose!"

He still orders an X-ray, to be sure.

"There's fluid in the gum," he says when he returns, "which is why it's loose. You have two options: You can—"

"Just pull it," I say. I already know the tooth is dead, and I can't afford a root canal.

"That's certainly the cheaper option," he says. "Are you sure?"

"Yes. Just pull it."

He numbs my gum, each needle a sharp pinch. Then he picks up a blunt-ended tool that looks almost like a screwdriver and levers it against the bottom of my tooth. I feel nothing, even after he pulls the tooth out of its socket with a cotton-ripping sound. He slips my molar into a blue autoclave packet—red strings of tissue still clinging to its root—and I almost ask if I can keep it. I imagine cracking it open with a hammer to expose the rot hidden inside.

He writes me prescriptions for an antibiotic and hydrocodone—for the pain. "You probably won't need it," he says with a shrug. "But just in case."

On the walk to the pharmacy, my father calls me from the shelter. He tells me about the Christmas loot "the bankers" gifted him:

two new shirts, socks, a pair of gloves, a scarf, a hat. He tells me he was lucky to be given a bed.

I ask him why around the wad of cotton wedged inside my mouth.

"The regulars were out, I guess. I'm not supposed to be here."

"Why not?"

"I don't have an ID with a local address," he says. "They're trying to get rid of their homeless population. Maybe I'll go down to South Carolina again; they got real good shelters down there. Showers and everything."

I wait. He waits, I know, for me to offer him a place to stay.

"Do you think," he begins slowly, "I could stay with you for a little while? I'm not drinking right now."

I remain silent. *I'll do it*, my mother had told me. *You just send him to me, and I'll take care of him.* But my mother is no longer here to take care of my dad.

"I don't know why I did what I did last week," my father says, to fill my silence. "I knew if I went back to Grandma's I was gonna get into trouble, but I did it anyway. Maybe I just needed to get out of there."

I sigh. "Why did you even start drinking to begin with?"

"I don't know," he says. "I went and saw your sister."

As if that was all the explanation I needed.

"I'll ask my roommates if it's okay," I say, hesitantly. No one ever taught me how to tell my father no.

"All right," he says, his voice picking up. "I'll go down to the train station and see how much a ticket is. Tuesdays—I think Tuesdays are the cheapest."

I walk home with my bundle of pills. My cat, Little Foot, follows me upstairs to our room. I close the door and set the two bottles—one an antibiotic, the other a painkiller—on my desk. I rotate the bottle of hydrocodone; read the label; uncap it; swallow a pill. I peel out of my clothes and turn off the light and burrow into a nest of blankets, and then I wait for the world to turn fuzzy and warm.

* * *

WHEN MARIE FIRST came to Boston to look for an apartment, I offered to let her stay with me. We hadn't talked much in the years since I left, but it felt good—comfortable—to talk with her again.

I told her about my ex, Marc, who briefly had moved into the apartment I shared with Nathan and a third roommate. I met Marc on a dating website, Geek 2 Geek, and in the beginning, our relationship was easy and sweet. I never talked about my family, or me.

We played videogames together. We watched *Battlestar Galactica* together from beginning to end. When he moved in, he bought a metal shelving unit and a grow lamp, and he started an indoor garden, planting tomatoes and peas. He tied twine above the rows of peas for their little hands to reach.

One summer, we visited Martha's Vineyard, where he had grown up and where his dad still lived. Marc's grandfather was visiting from California, and one night, the four of us went out in a metal dinghy to catch crabs under a full moon. We waded through waist-deep water and shone our flashlights across the bottom of the ocean floor. The crabs froze in the beams of light, and if the crabs were male—with blue-tipped claws instead of red—we slapped our aluminum nets over their heads and scooped them up with a turn of the wrist.

Back at the house, Marc and his father boiled the crabs while his grandfather and I sat next to each other and peeled the meat out of the shells. His grandfather was Chamorro, one of the indigenous peoples of Guam, and he told me stories from his island and from his time as an enlisted soldier in the U.S. Army that Marc had never heard before.

Another night, we visited one of his high school friends, a sanitation worker on the island. There were dozens of bottles of liquor—hundreds if not thousands of dollars' worth of alcohol—arranged in a circle in the middle of the living room floor. His friend had salvaged the bottles from the basement of a summer home that had flooded with sewage—the bottles were sealed, the contents safe, but the owners had thrown everything out.

That night, we both drank hard. But when he was drunk, Marc's eyes looked like my father's eyes, glistening shards of broken glass. I didn't want to talk to him—I didn't want to touch him—with eyes like that.

"I feel like I'm in prison," Marc complained one night after he had been drinking with his friends, who I refused to visit; they sat around a dark room, chain-smoked cigarettes, and discussed the conspiracy theories of Alex Jones. When he came home, I could still smell the beer and the smoke on his breath.

"I don't want to talk to you when you're drunk," I said, retreating to our bed.

"I feel like I'm not allowed to go out," he yelled, following me to our room.

I wouldn't look at him. I wouldn't talk to him. I shut down.

The next morning, he followed me from room to room and tried to start the conversation again, but each time, I stepped through a doorway and sheltered behind its walls. I could not be seen. I could not look into his face.

When he gave up on the conversation, I hid in our bedroom with my headphones on and a cat in my lap. He packed all his things—his computer and his clothes and his plants—and opened our bedroom only once, to tell me he was leaving and to collect his clothes. And then he left.

"It wasn't his fault," I told Marie. "Not really. I never told him what growing up with my father was like."

She asked me how my father was doing. She asked me about my grandmother and my sister. Sometime during the conversation, my roommate—a guy I met working at the thrift store—plopped down on the couch and eavesdropped on my family's drama.

"I'm sorry," my roommate interrupted finally, "but this is fascinating. I've never heard these things before."

Marie, surprised, looked between us, and I smiled a small smile. He wandered upstairs when the conversation drifted to Marie's family, to her mother and brothers and our old friends. But after he was gone, Marie stopped talking and slid her glasses over the crown of her head to pin her bangs out of her face. "I get it now," she said, pressing her fingertips over the tears in her eyes. "You came here to be alone."

Unexpectedly, I began to cry. I hadn't understood my own motivations until Marie gave voice to them.

If you isolate yourself long enough, you begin to believe no one can touch you. No one can take you back to the scared little girl you used to be. But one text, one letter, one phone call, that's all it really takes to prove you wrong.

MY FATHER BUYS a ticket and plans to arrive a few days after Christmas. My roommates—Marie and two of our other friends from college—are already familiar with the stories about my father, my family. Even knowing, when I ask if he can stay with us for a few days,they agree to let him sleep on the couch in a spare room downstairs.

Before either my grandmother or my father called, I'd scheduled a date with another guy from OkCupid for the night before Christmas Eve. I consider canceling, but I already canceled once, the night my tooth was pulled. Fuck it, I decide, and meet him at a restaurant near my apartment.

Sometime between the appetizer and the entrée, after he asks me about my ancestry, I start talking about my mother. When I realize where the conversation is going, I apologize and try to back out.

"It's okay," he insists. "I'm a really good listener."

After dinner, we go back to my apartment and watch the *Lady Gaga and the Muppets Holiday Spectacular.* "It's *so good,*" he insists.

Most of the songs are from her new album, which I didn't enjoy, and the show lacks a narrative arc. It is just Lady Gaga in different costumes with a dash of the Muppets thrown in for flavor. When he asks me what I think, I admit the Muppets and the texture of their felted faces fill me with anxiety, a feeling like ants marching up and down my spine.

After the show ends, he pries again into my mother's death; he asks me how she died, how I felt.

"I thought I was finally getting through it," I say. "And then my father's life falls apart."

He strokes my back, but I can't find comfort in it. I roll my shoulders uncomfortably, and he draws his hand away. "I'm getting tired," I say in apology.

"Oh, sure," he says, standing, as if to go. "I had a really great time tonight—you know, all things considered."

I thank him, but walk him to the door. "I just have a lot going on right now. I'm sorry."

"Don't worry," he insists, smiling. "I'd love to see you again."

I tell him I'll call.

I close the door and walk back upstairs. In bed, Little Foot wedges herself inside the crook of my arm. "I just want to die," I tell her, and when I say the words aloud, I begin to sob. I bury my face in the scruff of her neck, and she waits patiently for me to stop crying. "But if I die," I say finally, rubbing the bridge of her nose, "who would take care of you?"

CHRISTMAS MORNING, I take a bus to Nathan's to feed his cat while he is home for the holidays. On the kitchen table, I find a six-pack of Pepsi and one of the discs from *Buffy the Vampire Slayer* that I had left in his DVD player when I moved out. Rupert Giles's coquettish face gazes up at me, and a Post-it note tacked to the DVD reads, *"Thanks Danielle! -Goob."*

I feel the prickling kitten claws of Nathan's long-haired calico cat crawl up my leg, and I bend down to lift her onto my shoulder. I nuzzle my cheek into her soft rabbit fur and croon, "Hello, little Goob."

I carry her through the empty apartment, which has been repainted with mute shades of tan and white. When we first moved in, the kitchen had been a light shade of green, which reminded me of my mother's house in Florida, and the bathroom had been a rich goldenrod. I carry her into the living room, where two modern, plush sofas and an oversized loveseat dominate the floor space. Nathan's mother had given us a set of heavy wood-frame sofas that reminded me of the ones my family had in Florida in our brown-and-tan trailer, but his girlfriend hated them. His new couches came from Bob's Discount Furniture.

I sink down into one of the couches and let Goob pool into my lap. I scratch beneath her chin and smile at the soft vibration of her purrs. When I moved out, Nathan and I had been bickering. I left unwashed dishes in the sink and too many things in the living room. I didn't help enough around the house. He would leave for months every summer, on grant-funded trips to Canada and Texas to study bats, and expected me to take care of Goob. Whenever he was gone, she paced around the house and cried; lost weight; groomed obsessively, which created a bald patch near the base of her tail. My presence wasn't enough to calm her anxiety.

"She's a *cat*," he said, when I complained about his frequent, long absences. "They're self-reliant. They don't *need* people."

Nothing I said would have made him change his mind.

I toss Goob's fish around the living room and tell her I will be back.

It is already dark when I arrive home. I find a package on my porch—a gift from Nathan's mother, who, even after we broke up in college, has mailed me presents for every major and minor holiday. I pick up the package and the stack of mail off the floor and, under the porch light, flip through the envelopes addressed to past residents.

My downstairs neighbor's door cracks open an inch.

Startled, I glance up and smile. "Hi!" In the five months I've lived at the new apartment, we have never met before now.

He says nothing and closes the door.

I carry the package upstairs. Inside, I find Christmas-themed kitchen towels and potholders; a snowman-shaped marshmallow; two bars of soap made with goat's milk; a sheet of bird stickers; two packages of cat treats; a pair of hand-knit turquoise gloves. I pull out my phone and send Nathan a text message: *thx for sharing your mom.*

My date from OkCupid texts me a photo of his sister's cats batting balls of wrapping paper around the floor. *Hope you had a great holiday!* he says, adding that he would love to see me again.

I draft and delete a number of responses. *I don't think I'm up for hanging out,* I finally reply. *I'm pretty wrecked this week, sorry.*

MY EX, MARC, sent me a Facebook message a few days after my mother died. *I'm just gonna throw this out there, but if you need someone to vent to, I'm here,* he had said, adding, *I know you're not big on all that.*

At the time, I thanked him and declined his offer. But after my father buys his bus ticket, I text Marc and ask if he's free to hang out.

Whatever works for you, he says.

I MEET MY father at South Station. I wait on the platform and watch him walk off the train—shoulders back, feet fast. He carries a single black bag. When he stops in front of me, he smiles, sad. "You look like your mom, standing there like that."

I wonder what he means—what part of her he sees in me—but don't ask. I hug him, ginger.

"Let me smoke a cigarette before we get on the train," he says, "I'm dying."

I follow him through the station and wait quietly as he smokes one of his rolled cigarettes. Then I show him the way home, where I pull a sheet over the couch cushions and offer him one of the blankets my grandmother crocheted.

We sit down next to each other, and he unpacks his bag, showing me the new socks and underwear the bankers gifted him for Christmas. He pulls out his netbook and says, "I thought I could work on my apps while I'm here."

My father originally learned to write Android apps to create a program he claimed could predict the best lottery numbers to play. The app had decent reviews, but after my nephew was diagnosed with autism, my father began creating kids' apps instead. He showed me one of the new apps he was working on, *Kids Farm Animals*, a simple farm game with three different scenes. In one, a frog hops from lily pad to lily pad; the shadow of a fish glides under the surface of the pond. If you touch the shadow, the fish flips into the air in surprise. In another, you can pick carrots out of a field, and my father's voice—warped digitally, but still recognizable—counts *one, two, three* as you go. A groundhog sits beside the field, and if you don't knock him out, he steals all the carrots, which resets the counter to zero. In the last, an owl pops its head out of a barn.

"I showed Sebastian an early version of this one," my father says, "but the owl didn't hoot yet. He'd push on the owl, and he knew something was supposed to happen, so he got all frustrated. He handed it back to me and kept saying, 'Hoot! Hoot!'" My father laughs. "He knew it was supposed to hoot, but I couldn't fix it that fast."

I laugh, too. The last time I visited home, my nephew hadn't been very interested in me, but he knew how to ask my father for a peanut butter cracker, or for his Kindle to be charged, or for the last fifteen seconds of a movie to be replayed, without a word. I took a picture of them together: My nephew lies upside down in my father's lap, his legs propped up against my father's chest, his toes curled around my father's chin.

"All the money from these apps is going into a bank account for Sebastian," my father says.

"You're a good grandpa."

"He's really smart," he continues, as if he hasn't heard me. "His teachers think he's a savant. He's going to be smarter than all of us."

The doorbell rings, and I jump off the couch. "One second," I tell my father, then run downstairs to the front door.

Marc, wearing a pair of black dress pants and the same blue-and-gray jacket he owned when we were together two years before, stands on the porch. He holds a styrofoam Dunkin' Donuts cup and rolls his shoulders in a nervous shrug. "Hey," he says.

"Hi," I say, pressing myself against the wall. "Come in."

He follows me upstairs, and my father stands up to greet him.

"Do you remember Marc?" I ask. Marc drove me down to Pennsylvania one early summer, and he had met both my grandmother and my dad. I took him to the fruit farm where I worked as a kid, and we bought a pint of black raspberries to eat in the car.

"Yeah," my father says, extending his hand. "How you doing?"

"Hi, Mike," Marc says, shaking hands.

"I'm gonna smoke a cigarette and go to bed," my father says. "I'm tired." He picks up his bag of tobacco and walks past us, toward the door.

"It's past your bedtime," I try to joke.

He laughs a small laugh.

I show Marc upstairs to my room.

"Oh my god," he laughs, "how is it so cold up here?"

I crawl under the blankets and pat the spot beside me. "The insulation is terrible, and we keep the heat turned down to save money."

Marc slides in beside me; we lie on our backs, side by side. I shiver, a tremor that makes my teeth chatter quietly. I'm not sure if it's from the cold or my nerves.

"How are you doing?" he asks, glancing at me out of the corner of his eye.

"Things are so crazy right now," I say. "It wasn't just that my mom died. There was all this other—shit. And it all happened so fast."

"That's hard," he says, quiet.

I tell him about the trip to Florida—about Dale, and the things I found. How alone I had been. How Eileen disappeared. How my father was homeless and my responsibility again. I walk backward in time, telling him things I never told him about my childhood, because my heartache feels rooted in more than the last three months of my life. I start crying and roll away from him to bury my face in my hands.

He moves closer and wraps his arms around my waist and hugs me against him. "I'm sorry," he says, leaning his head against mine. "I didn't know there was so much."

"I just want to die," I breathe.

Marc holds me tighter. "Please don't do that," he whispers, urgently. "Please don't do that."

I shake my head against his. When my tears finally stop, I turn slowly to face him. "I think I told you more tonight than I did the entire time we were dating," I laugh.

"It puts a lot of things into perspective."

"What do you mean?"

He rolls onto his back again and drapes his arm over his eyes. "It makes me feel terrible about the way things ended."

"That wasn't your fault," I say.

I hug one of my blankets tighter around my shoulders, pinning it against the bed to create a flimsy barrier between his body and mine. Our conversation feels like it's heading in a dangerous direction. "I don't know if I'm ready to date anyone," I tell him, worried I will break his heart.

"I know," he says. He slides his arm under the blanket and hugs me closer. "I'm just happy to be here right now. I'm not going to pressure you into anything."

"Thank you, Marc," I whisper, resting my head on his chest. I fall asleep listening to the soft, rapid beating of his heart.

Marc leaves for work early the next morning. By the time I come downstairs for breakfast, my father has been awake for hours. He watches me pour a bowl of cereal.

"Did he come over because of me?" he asks. His voice, small and quiet.

Something swells in my throat. "Of course not," I say, trying not to cry. Is he worried I am scared of him? Of what he might do? "I asked him to come over before you even bought your ticket."

"Oh," he says.

I HAVE THE entire week off work after the holidays, through the new year. My father and I begin watching *Battlestar Galactica*, the remake. I decide to make a homemade dinner. I order a pork shoulder from the grocer, an eight-and-a-half pound slab of pig that lands heavily on my counter the next day. "What am I going to do with this?" I ask my dad, turning the package in a slow circle. "This is never going to fit in my crockpot."

"We'll just have to chop her up," my father titters, digging through my kitchen drawers. He finds a knife and starts hacking, pulling chunks of meat away from the bone.

I collect the bits of meat in a bowl and rub them with salt and pepper and paprika, according to a recipe I find online.

"You could feed this to the dog across the street," my father says, wielding the bone.

"Or we could make a stock," I say, though I have never made a stock before.

"You really are a fancy chef now," he says.

I laugh. "No. I just have the Internet."

I find a recipe for pork stock, then another for homemade pork and beans. My father offers to walk down to the grocery store and returns with two bags of dried navy beans.

I message Marc and asks him if he wants to come over for dinner, and he says yes.

I bake a pan of fresh cornbread, and by some great miracle, everything is done cooking when Marc arrives. The three of us sit down in the living room to watch *Battlestar Galactica*, but my father and Marc keep talking over the show.

"This never used to happen," Marc laughs. "She never used to cook." The entire time we lived together, Marc cooked every meal I didn't order from Foodler.

"I remember when she couldn't even boil water," my father says, then laughs. "Marc's never going to leave if you keep feeding him like this."

"Just watch the show," I beg.

The next day, my father leaves early for work: He wants to pick up a few hours at the labor hall. He had to borrow money from Sebastian's bank account to buy the ticket to Boston, and he wants to put the money back as soon as he can. The labor hall sends him to an office in Cambridge to install new cubicles, and even though he only works for two hours, they pay him for a half day. He rescues a like-new office chair from the Dumpster and rides it home on the train, rolling around one of the metal poles with the movement of the car.

A snowstorm hits that week, and my father's phone chirps incessantly with offer after offer to shovel snow. He didn't bring enough cold-weather clothing, so we take a quick trip to my favorite thrift store and dig through the dollar-a-pound pile for used sweatshirts.

Before he leaves for work in the morning, I pack him lunch— pulled pork sandwiches and a container of beans—but after the end of his first long day, he complains of muscle aches.

The next morning, I pack him a banana.

When he comes home, he lays the banana in front of me—its skin black and shriveled. "I killed your banana," he says.

"What happened?" I gasp, laughing.

"I think it was the cold!"

It feels good to play house with my dad. Even after I return to work, we spend every evening together. We watch *BSG*, and sometimes, my father tells me stories—not the ones I remember from childhood, but stories I have never heard before. I close my eyes to listen—to write new memories over the old. He tells me about working for his brother's company, which hired him to perform maintenance on large mainframe computers, like the PDP-10 and the Foonly F1. The names make me laugh. My uncle sold the computers to colleges and businesses both in and out of California, which was how my father ended up in Prescott, where he met my mother. But he wasn't ready to talk about my mother yet.

I realize I missed him, but also that we had never spent so much time together when he was sober.

I am sad when my father decides to leave. He made enough money to buy a ticket back to Pennsylvania and to rent a motel room for a week. He tells me he misses my nephew, who he watches most weekends, but says that if he can't find work in York, he might go back to South Carolina, where it's warm. He feels too old to sleep outside in the cold anymore.

We don't have time to finish watching *Battlestar Galactica* before he leaves. We watch the end of the first season, then agree to watch the final episode. I worry the heavy-handed religiosity of the show's finale will disappoint him, but he cheers out loud when the rebel Centurions are given their own Basestar.

"Maybe they'll come pick me up and I can get a fighter pilot girlfriend," he jokes.

A few hours after he leaves, he sends me a text: *Made the train ok but still no sign of Centurions.*

A few days later, he calls me from my uncle's cellphone, but I immediately hang up. I can tell from the sound of his voice that he is already drinking again.

Nobody is ever

❖

IN THE SILENCE my father's absence creates, I begin writing about my mother. I call out of work and write for twelve, fourteen, fifteen hours a day. I write about our childhood. I write about the days I spent in her hospital room. I open the box of her possessions and begin writing around the things I find. I am like Christopher Columbus discovering the Americas—laying claim to things that are not mine.

Each time I finish a section, I print it out and mail it to Eileen. She tells me the guards recognize her mail by how thick the envelopes are. She worries she sounds like an addict; she worries what people will think of her. But she tells me she has been sharing the pages with her fellow inmates—that they think it's good—and she encourages me to keep writing. She asks me to consider fictionalizing the story, but writing the truth, or my understanding of it, is the only path I can see through the weeds.

Merry Christmas & Happy
B-Day

XOX OXOXOXOXOXOXO XOXO
XOXOXOXOX OXOXO XOXO
    please call
P.S. From Fran
    Not collect!!!
    thank you

Merry X-mas & Happy New Year

        Love Always,
        Danielle

Within this greeting, Mother,
There's special love for you
And special wishes that your day
Is happy, through and through,
And, as you read the message,
Just hope you'll smile a bit
And think of all the loving thoughts
That come along with it.

Love Eileen

TITLE: A card sent from Eileen and Danielle Geller to "Tweety" Lee.

DATE: circa December 1997

TYPE OF RESOURCE: birthday cards

DESCRIPTION: A card sent from two daughters for their mother's birthday and Christmas with a request for her to call, but not collect. The card doesn't say much, but in Lee's diary from December 12, 1997, she writes, "I received a Birthday Card from Danielle. I burst into tears and thought of how much I miss the two of them and how much are bound is still there. I Love Them So!"

TITLE: "Tweety" Lee, pregnant with Alexandra, sits on Tony's lap and kisses him over her shoulder.

DATE: circa May 1998

TYPE OF RESOURCE: color photographs

DESCRIPTION: Lee and Tony day drink on a porch with their friends. Months pregnant, my mother curls her fingers around the neck of a brown bottle. My father always bragged that he never let her drink when she was pregnant with us, but my mother tells me when I am older that she still drank wine coolers, because the doctor said it was okay.

TITLE: "Tweety" Lee holds her newborn daughter, Alexandra, on the porch.

DATE: circa May 1998

TYPE OF RESOURCE: color photographs

DESCRIPTION: Smiling, Lee poses with her newborn daughter, Alexandra, swaddled in a white cloth with an indiscernible blue pattern. She sits on the back porch of the house she shares with her boyfriend, Tony.

TITLE: "Tweety" Lee and her daughters Danielle and Eileen Geller embrace.

DATE: 1999

TYPE OF RESOURCE: color photographs

DESCRIPTION: My mother surprises me and my sister in front of our apartment building in Yoe, Pennsylvania. After our initial shock, the three of us hug one another and cry. My grandmother takes a photograph of us, the straight sidewalks, the tidy lawns.

TITLE: "Tweety" Lee and her daughters sit at the kitchen table with a stack of childhood photographs.

DATE: 1999

TYPE OF RESOURCE: color photographs

DESCRIPTION: My mother brought us a gift of childhood photographs, of me and my sister as toddlers at our apartment on Nokomis Avenue. She labels the photos in her neat cursive as we talk. My sister smiles, her teeth showing. My parakeet, Ripple, sits happily on my mother's shoulder. I bundle myself in two blankets and appear pale and tired.

TITLE: "Tweety" Lee and husband, Ron Sims, celebrate their wedding at Sneakers.

DATE: 2003

TYPE OF RESOURCE: color photographs

DESCRIPTION: My mother and Ron celebrate their wedding at Sneakers, their favorite dive bar. Ron feeds a piece of cake to my laughing mother; there is icing on the tip of her nose. My mother did not tell me she was getting married, and she did not invite us to the wedding. I did not meet him until after they were already divorced.

TITLE: Eileen and Michael Geller pose together in Eileen's apartment.

DATE: 2008

TYPE OF RESOURCE: color photographs

DESCRIPTION: Eileen and my father pose together for a photograph; my sister smiles. They each hold a bottle of beer. My father wears a blue shirt with the words THE FRIENDLY BUNCH across the front.

TITLE: Michael Geller gropes "Tweety" Lee while drinking in their daughter
Eileen's apartment.

DATE: 2008

TYPE OF RESOURCE: color photographs

DESCRIPTION: Eileen takes a photograph of our parents. They are still smiling and laughing and have not yet had too much to drink. My mother wears
red nail polish. The scar from my father's spiral fracture is visible on his left
shin.

III

a woman without her people
a woman who can never return home
is crazy with grief
and always longing

I am that woman
even the crazy moon is lonely

—DEBRA MAGPIE EARLING, *The Lost Journals of Sacajawea*

I woke up with a dream about me & mom & dad & Christmas and how the light of God pulling me into the life that is now teaching what I have to do.

❖

THE DAY I flew to Albuquerque to meet my mother's family, the entire United States seemed to be smothered beneath a single dark cloud. Occasionally, the cloud cover broke, allowing the sun to shine on patches of the winter-brown earth below. As a little girl, I imagined these pillars of light were sent from God—each sunbeam a conveyor, lifting souls to heaven. But I had not believed that in a long time.

When I called to tell my grandmother about finding my mother's family, about the memorial service we would be holding on the reservation, she asked me not to tell my sister. "She'll just get upset," she said.

I had already sent Eileen a letter telling her about the trip. I had already packed paper and envelopes to mail her another letter while I was there. "I'm not going to lie to her," I told my grandmother.

"I just don't see a reason to upset her," Grandma complained.

I imagined the news *would* upset Eileen. I imagined she would be hurt to miss out. But I had just begun to earn my sister's trust, and I could not risk losing it again to keep my grandmother's version of peace.

A FEW WEEKS earlier, at a midwinter gathering of the American Library Association in Philadelphia, I stumbled across a Navajo jewelry vendor, an elder with graying black hair, with a booth in the main exhibition hall. I lingered at the booth and, sliding her rings on and off my fingers, watched her interact with another conference attendee.

"I just *love* Native jewelry," the attendee said, holding a squash blossom necklace in the air.

The Navajo woman nodded and smiled politely, but the woman left the necklace on the table and walked farther down the row. I waited to see if she would recognize me as like her; if she would ask me about my family. But she remained silent and watched my hands.

"My mother was Navajo," I said, finally.

The woman said, "Oh," in a noncommittal way.

"She died in September," I said without meaning to.

She apologized but seemed to be looking elsewhere.

Nervously, I walked my fingers over the rows of rings and necklaces and bracelets in their black velvet cases. I had intruded, but I needed to find a way in. I didn't imagine she knew my mother's family; I didn't even imagine she cared. But I had reached the limits of my documentary sleuthing—the letters from my mother's family were old, the addresses and phone numbers ancient—and this jeweler seemed like my last chance. "I haven't been able to get in touch with her family on the reservation," I said, "to tell them she died."

"You should put an obituary in the *Navajo Times*," she offered. "Everyone reads the *Navajo Times*."

Feeling suddenly very stupid, I said, "I should have known that." It hadn't made sense to me to place an obituary in a Florida newspaper, but I should have thought to write one for her family on the reservation.

The woman said nothing.

My hands kept returning to the same ring—fourteen skinny beads of turquoise arranged in a diamond pattern on a thin silver band. "I'd like this one," I said, setting the ring in front of her.

After I paid for the ring, I left the conference and returned to my hotel room. I looked up other obituaries that had been placed on the *Navajo Times* website and followed their format as best I could: Most of the obituaries included a person's blood clans, but the family tree my mother had left me was in my apartment in Boston, and I had never committed my blood clans to memory. I included her name and the nickname her family gave her, Tweety. I included the day she was born and the day she died. I included the names of her surviving family: me, my sister, and my nephew. I included the names of her parents, who were already deceased, and the name of her sister, whose name—I would learn later—I misremembered. I asked the editor to include my contact information—my name, my email address, and my phone number—so that her family could reach me. I could feel the nervous pulse of my heart in my fingertips as I clicked Send.

An entire day passed, and I heard nothing.

I returned to Boston from the conference and waited a second day, and a third. Nothing.

On the fourth day, I received a call from an Arizona number. A man's voice asked, "Is this Danielle?"

I said yes.

"You're Tweety's daughter?"

"Yes," I said again.

He told me he lived across the street from my aunt—that he had watched my mother and her siblings grow up. "I found your number in the *Navajo Times*," he said, "but I'm a little confused. I got a Christmas card from your mother two months ago."

"That's not possible," I said, but I instantly began to doubt—not that he knew my mother, not that we were talking about the same Laureen "Tweety" Lee but, magically, that my mother was dead. When I closed my eyes, I imagined her alive, sitting in the Florida sun. Could she still be alive? Could she be hiding from me? Could the last five months have been a dream?

His voice interrupted me. "What happened?" he asked.

"She had a heart attack," I said, rejecting the dream.

"A heart attack?" He sounded skeptical.

I explained that my mother had been drinking a lot before she died—that when she tried to stop, she died from withdrawal.

He offered to give me my aunt's number, but I didn't call my mother's sister immediately. I was too worried she would be angry with me—I should have found her earlier. I walked back to my desk and sat in front of my computer and stared at the screen, but it was impossible to get any work done.

I walked into the stairwell and stared out the window at a black metal sculpture, *La Grande Voile,* that reminded me of a six-legged cat.

I dialed the number the man gave me. I introduced myself as Tweety's eldest daughter, the one who had placed the obituary in the paper.

The woman who answered sounded exactly like my mother— her voice lilting, with all the hard consonants dropped at the ends of her words. But she sounded angry; she demanded to know what had happened.

I repeated the story of how my mother died. My throat felt tight with the well of tears I held back.

"I don't understand. What *happened?*" she asked again.

There was a period of time when my mother was dead, but my aunt's sister was still alive and walking her mother's red earth. I could not reconcile that time. "I'm so sorry," I said. "I didn't know how to get ahold of you. The numbers I had were old, and I could only find a post office box number."

"We don't have street addresses out here," she sighed, exasperated already with the things I didn't know. "I should have *known.*"

"I'm sorry," I said again.

My mother's sister began to cry. I waited, silent.

"We have to do something for her," she said, her tears stopping abruptly; the anger falling out of her voice. "A memorial."

"Yeah, of course," I agreed.

"Can you come out?" she asked. "Next week, maybe? The family can help."

I hesitated; I hadn't expected her to want to see me so soon. And I had taken so much time off work already—called out so many days—I wasn't sure my boss would approve, but I knew I needed to meet my mother's family more than I needed a job. I told her I would try.

She sighed. "I need to go. I'm at work. But I'll call you later," she said, adding, "Okay, baby?" the way my mother always did.

I nodded and told her okay.

"You're not alone," she said, ending the call.

I set my phone on the window ledge and felt my throat relax. I buried my face in my hands and let the tears arrive.

I CALLED MARC from the train and quickly told him about the obituary and the conversation with my aunt.

"Wow," he said. "Are you going to go?"

"I don't know," I said. "I'm going to try, I guess?" I had asked my boss if I could take the time off work; I assured him I wouldn't fall behind on my projects, and he had given me his blessing.

"Maybe I could take some time off," Marc said, thinking aloud. "We could drive out there—make a trip of it."

"I don't think there's enough time. She wants to do it next week." I didn't tell him that I wanted to make the journey alone.

"Oh," he said, sounding disappointed. "Yeah, I can't get off work with that short notice."

"It's okay," I said, relieved.

MY AUNT CALLED me later that night. She told me she had checked the card my mother sent for Christmas. The sound of a can cracking open punctuated the end of her sentence, and I held my breath. "Dale wrote something on the back," she said. "'May she rest in peace.' I didn't know what it meant."

"He *what*?" I asked, trying not to scream. "He told me he didn't know how to contact you."

"He didn't even write to tell me what happened," she said.

I was grateful he hadn't—that I had been the one, at least, to tell her. Relief, followed by guilt. I didn't notice the silence on the phone until my aunt started talking again.

"I'm just sitting outside in my truck," she said. "It makes me so sad."

I could picture her then. I recognized the open, empty sound that surrounded her; felt the comfortable weight of the night air, like a thick quilt. I longed to be there.

She wanted to hold the memorial service the following Friday, but she asked me to come out early, to stay a week. I agreed. The plane ticket was outrageously expensive on such short notice, but I didn't hesitate to buy it after we hung up the phone. It was just one more addition to my ballooning credit-card debt. I started packing, folding my clothes into my mother's suitcase, the one I had found in her closet in Florida, the one that had held all of her things.

EVEN THE BOOK I brought with me on the plane could not distract me from thoughts of my mother, or that final day with her in the hospital. I remembered the feel of her skin, mortuary cold—a too-visceral reminder that the critical systems of her body were failing.

The hospice worker had given me a folder of information about their hospice program, an advertisement for cremation services, and pamphlets on death and dying. The pamphlets offered token pieces of end-of-life advice: that it is not unusual for your loved one to linger; that in order to let go, your loved one needs to know the people they are leaving behind will be okay; that it is important to say goodbye.

I was not convinced I believed in spirits, or that there was any presence in my mother's body that understood what I might say. But I felt compelled to say something.

I scanned my mind for every movie or television cliché I could remember. "It's okay to let go," I began, self-consciously keeping my eye on the hallway. "I know you loved me, and Eileen. I know you did your best."

But even as I said the words, I doubted them. Why should I tell my mother what I thought she wanted to hear?

"I'm glad I'm the one here," I said, lowering my voice. I let the air I had been holding in the deepest part of my lungs out, in one foul breath. "I never told you what I meant to say. I never did anything because of you, only despite you. I am nothing like you, and I'm grateful for it."

I waited. I wasn't sure what I was waiting for. There was no sign—no sudden twitch of her lips, no holy corona, no voice from above—to make me believe anyone or anything had heard me. I didn't feel unburdened, only vindictive and cruel.

"I'll be okay," I sighed, finally. "You should go." But I knew the machines and the drugs were holding her there, and the decision could not be made by her body alone.

AS THE PLANE began its descent over the Sandia Foothills, down below the cloud cover, I distracted myself with the view out the window. I scanned the snow-covered ridges and paths between the conifer trees for any sign of movement, but all was still. The mountains transitioned to flat brown desert, and my eyes traced the veins of snowmelt and rainwater that had cut deep grooves in the earth.

My cousin waited for me at the gate. There was something about her—the shape of her eyes, or her shameless smile—that reminded me of Eileen. "You sounded white on the phone," my cousin said, seeming surprised, "but you look like your mom!"

I laughed, and we hugged. "You look like my sister," I said.

My cousin's neighbor, an old white man who called himself Shorty, waited for us near the exit. He was the man who first called me after I posted the obituary—he had watched my mother and her brothers and sister grow up. As he walked to his truck, he told

me he came to the reservation as an engineer, working at one of
the uranium plants, but met and married a Navajo woman, and so
he stayed.

We left Albuquerque, all pink concrete and metal painted turquoise blue, and drove north along I-40. The airport was a two-
hour drive from where my family lived on the reservation, and my
cousin spent most of the drive on her phone. The land around us
turned brown and gray, though the sandstone mesas in the distance
were streaked with shades of red and white. It started to flurry, but
the snow wouldn't stick.

As we drove, Shorty named some of the towns and geologic
features in Navajo. "That's Tsoodził," he said, pointing toward a
distant, snow-capped peak. "Can you say that?"

"Soo—" I tried. "Sooo—"

"Mount Taylor," he laughed. "That's one of the four sacred
mountains."

"Oh," I said.

Closer to the reservation, we passed the casino, a solid structure
that looked more like a multipeaked white tent.

My cousin leaned forward and whispered into my ear, "That
place is full of skin-walkers."

"What's a skin-walker?" I asked.

She gasped. "You don't know what skin-walkers are?"

I shook my head and glanced at Shorty, suddenly silent in the
driver's seat.

"We have skin-walkers out here," my cousin said, wedging her
shoulders between Shorty and me. "They're witches. They can
turn into animals, and they curse people. And that's where they all
hang out."

I laughed, which I immediately realized was the wrong thing to
do. I tried to turn my laugh into a cough. "Do you believe in skin-
walkers?" I asked Shorty.

My cousin eased herself into the back seat.

Shorty cleared his throat. "You hear stories," he said, but that was all he would say.

We stopped in Gallup for groceries—my aunt wouldn't have anything to eat, Shorty claimed. By the time we reached my aunt's neighborhood, the sun was already beginning to set.

I VISITED THE reservation only once when I was a child, when I was three years old. My mother and my father packed my younger sister, my cat, and me into a car to drive from Florida to Window Rock, Arizona, to visit my mother's family on the reservation and to register me and my sister with the Navajo Nation. The cat jumped out of the car somewhere in Texas, and my father was bitten on the leg by a brown recluse spider, and he was arrested on an old warrant and did a stint in jail, but we made it to the reservation otherwise intact.

My memories of that visit are small but incremental: a yellow butterfly in a jar on a windowsill; the warmth of the rust-colored earth; an old junker resting beside a fence. I pulled a wiper blade off the car and sliced open my inner thigh—a lasting scar, a pale recession.

My grandmother tells me I hated the reservation. When I came home, she said I sat in her kitchen and cried because my mother's mother locked me in a dark closet while my mother went out drinking with her old friends. That my uncles scared me with their masks.

Years later, when I asked my mother about that trip, about the masks my uncles wore, she laughed. "I can't believe you remembered that!" She told me they wore Halloween masks, a gorilla and a witch.

I DIDN'T RECOGNIZE my grandmother's house with its little white porch, or the yard out front, or the road, pocked with wide potholes.

My aunt was still at work when we arrived, so my cousin and I waited at Shorty's. She sprawled in a recliner by the kitchen table, as if at home, and Shorty scolded her, "Don't sit with your pussy hanging out."

My cousin laughed and rolled her eyes, and when I looked at her, she shrugged. "He's just a dirty ol' man."

Still, I was relieved when my aunt showed up. I ran to the door to meet her, a woman as short and round as my mother. She wore a simple sweatshirt and jeans and a pair of black biker boots, but her hair was dyed and highlighted a dirty blonde, which reminded me of my sister. She started crying as soon as she saw me, and she pulled me into a hug.

The three of us sat at Shorty's table, and he fed us fried chicken and potato salad. "When is the memorial service?" he asked.

"Friday," my aunt said.

Shorty cleared his throat. "We all know Tweety had her faults," he said, "but I think the two of you should celebrate her life. There's no need to dwell on all the rest."

"I know," my aunt said, the tears creeping back into her eyes.

I pushed the potato salad around on my plate.

After dinner, I followed my aunt across the street to my grandmother's house. The living room was dark; smaller than I imagined, somehow. There were Pendleton blankets draped over the couch and loveseat. One doorway led to the kitchen, and another to a room with a wood-burning stove.

"You're going to share my room," my cousin said, leading me down a short hall. She flicked on the light and walked over to a plastic cage. "This is my hamster!" she chirped, opening the top of the cage and cradling a ping-pong ball of fur in her hands. She held him toward me and smiled. "Isn't he cute?"

I watched the hamster nose at the crevices between her fingers and laughed. "Yes."

My aunt, opening a can of beer, appeared in the doorway. "We're meeting with the priest at ten tomorrow morning to go over the service," she said, "but I'm going to go cruise with my friends."

It didn't sound like I was invited, but I told her I was tired and just wanted to go to bed.

We woke in the middle of the night to my aunt shouting my cousin's name.

My cousin stirred and groaned loudly, "What!"

"Your hamster is out of its cage again!" she hollered back.

Throwing off her blankets, my cousin disappeared into her mother's room. A few minutes later, she returned, switching on the light with the cage of her hands. "It's broken," she mumbled, dumping the hamster back in its cage. She wiggled the door around until she felt it was locked, then turned off the light and climbed back into bed.

We woke again to my aunt shouting her name.

When my cousin didn't respond, my aunt flew into the room. "Your hamster escaped!" she yelled, turning on the lights.

Reluctantly, my cousin rolled out of bed. I lifted my head and listened to a rummaging sound in her mother's closet, which must have been connected to her own. "I can't find it," I heard my cousin complain before returning to bed.

I woke again to the sound of small teeth chewing on something like cardboard. I rolled over and whispered, sleepily, "I think your hamster is back in its cage."

"No, it's not!" she yelled, jumping out of bed and turning on the light. She dove into her closet to find it, and I sat up. As she threw clothes from one side of her closet to the other, I watched the hamster dart between her feet and toward the dresser.

"It's behind you!" I yelled.

My cousin spun on her knees and pounced on it with both hands. She stood and dropped it into its cage.

"Does this happen every night?" I asked.

"No," she laughed, turning off the light.

My aunt was the first one awake the next morning. When I walked into the kitchen, she was cooking bacon and eggs. She raised her head from behind the open refrigerator door and handed me a block of bright-orange cheese. "Have you ever had commodity cheese?" she asked.

"No," I said, hefting the cheese in my hand. It looked a little bit like Velveeta.

"It's so *good*," my cousin gasped from behind me, and she snatched the cheese from my hand. She grated a large pile on top of her eggs, then handed it back to me.

I was more conservative. It was a little milky, a little rubbery.

"Do you like it?" my cousin asked.

"Yeah," I said, hoping she couldn't hear the lie.

My aunt sat across from us at the table and glanced back and forth between us. "You guys are sisters," she said. "In the Navajo culture, you're sisters through your grandmother."

I had read about this when I had taken a few anthropology classes as an undergraduate. The clan system was a system of familial relationships, and our blood clans were inherited along the maternal line. My first clan was my mother's mother's clan; my second, my father's mother's. The Navajo language has more words than English for all the tangles of a family tree, but the way I understood it, the people who also shared my blood clan were considered my close relations—my sisters and brothers, my aunts and uncles—even if we did not know how or through whom we were related. But before I met my aunt and my cousin, I hadn't connected the dots about what this meant for me.

"You're sisters," my aunt repeated, "and you're my daughter now. I'm your little mother. You have a lot of family out here."

I nodded and smiled at my cousin, who had felt like a sister to me from the moment we met.

"Your blood clan is the Tsi'naajinii," my aunt continued. "You say, I'm born to the Tsi'naajinii, born for the Bilagáana."

My cousin-sister looked up at her mother. "I have the same clans, huh, Mom?"

"Yes," she said.

My cousin-sister smiled at me. "My dad's white, too."

Suddenly, my aunt leapt out of her chair and yelled, "We have to meet the priest!"

"I'll get dressed fast," I said.

Minutes later, we were in the truck, pulling out of the backyard. I noticed a large bird with a black-and-white speckled chest perched in the tree above the driveway.

"What are you looking at?" my cousin-sister asked.

"A bird," I said, leaning forward to watch him through the windshield until he was out of sight.

MY GRANDPARENTS AND their children converted to Catholicism when my mother was in high school. They were baptized at St. Michael's, a Catholic mission, and my aunt decided to hold the memorial service there. The sandstone church sat atop a squat hill. As we followed the drive, a small pack of rez dogs chased a squirrel across the yard and up a tree.

The priest invited us into a small room, empty except for a large wooden table and chairs. My aunt sat down next to the priest, and my cousin-sister and I claimed chairs across from them. The priest opened a pocket-sized notebook and began clicking his pen. "First, I'd like to learn a little about your mother, so I can say a few words about her. Her name was Laureen Lee—what was her middle name?"

"Pearl," I answered, glancing at my aunt. "And her family called her Tweety."

My cousin-sister looked up from her phone. "That's cause she talked too much, huh, Mom?"

"Yes," my aunt said.

I glanced between my aunt and my cousin-sister; that wasn't the reason as I understood it, but I stayed quiet.

"And what were some of her roles?" the priest asked. "She was a mother, obviously. A sister. Was she married?"

"Yes," I said, but then shook my head. "But he passed away."

"What was his name?" he asked.

I hesitated. I didn't want Ron to be part of this. "They divorced before he passed away."

"Ooookay," the priest said, slowly. He seemed unwilling to press me, at least. "What was her occupation?"

My aunt looked at me.

"She had a couple jobs. She was a waitress when I was a kid. She worked in construction for a little while." I clasped my hands on the tabletop. "She sold orchids at a road stand."

My cousin-sister smiled at me. "She told me that—that she was selling flowers."

I tilted my head in her direction and wondered how often she and my mother talked.

"What were some things she was good at?" he asked.

I expected my aunt to interject, but she stayed silent, watching me. I frantically searched my memories. My mother was good at coloring—she always colored in close circles, always stayed inside the lines. But that wasn't what he meant. I remembered my conversations with Dale—that she took care of him when he had cancer. I remembered a letter she had written to one of her cousins about her desire to take care of her father when he was sick. And I remembered her promise to take care of my father after my grandmother was gone. "She was good at taking care of people," I said.

The priest glanced at me over the rim of his glasses. "So, she was a caregiver."

I thought of how she had neglected her care of my sisters and me, but nodded agreement. "Yes."

"What kind of music did she like?" he asked.

I thought back to the rows of cassette tapes I left in Dale's house. I remembered the strange glamour shot of the mustachioed man in the cowboy hat. "Country," I guessed.

"I was going to say that," my cousin-sister said.

"What was your favorite meal that she cooked for you?"

McDonald's? Mac and cheese? I thought back to the time I visited her in Florida and the meal she cooked for Ron—the meal I didn't eat. "Liver and onions," I said.

"Wow," he laughed. "If she could make liver and onions taste good, she must have been an amazing cook."

"Our mom used to cook it," my aunt chimed in.

The priest tucked his notebook back into his front pocket and shifted the stack of books in front of him. There would be three readings, he explained—one from the Old Testament, and two from the New—one of which would be from the Gospels. He would select the passage from the Gospels.

We nodded.

"I recommend Wisdom 4:7–15 for those who pass at a young age," he said, tilting the book toward him as he read. "The virtuous man, though he die before his time, will find rest. Length of days is not what makes age honorable, nor number of years the true measure of life . . ."

My aunt and I glanced at each other across the table. She shook her head. "Another."

The priest cleared his throat. "I like this one because it measures success not by age but by what someone accomplished in the years they had on this earth—"

I shook my head. "Another."

The priest began reading a passage from the book of Wisdom. I tried hard to listen. "Their going looked like a disaster," he droned, "their leaving us, like annihilation."

Annihilation. The word caught in my chest. Her leaving *had* been annihilation—past and present and future, she was gone, and I was defeated. I looked at my aunt and found tears mirrored in our eyes. The words were heavy, overstated, but apt.

"That one?" my aunt asked, wiping her eyes.

"That one," I said.

The priest moved on to passages from the New Testament, but I stopped being able to focus on the words. The New Testament God carried less weight than the vengeful God of the Old.

"I'll make a photocopy of these for you," the priest offered as he stood. "Whoever reads them should practice a few times before the service."

"Thank you, Father," my aunt said.

After he left the room, my cousin-sister's eyes slanted toward us over her phone. "I want to ask him a question," she said.

"What?" her mother asked.

"If God exists," she giggled.

Her mother sighed and stood, shaking her head. She followed the priest out of the room to settle the cost of the service, and my cousin-sister and I drifted outside. I turned in circles, surveying the trees that bordered the parking lot until my eye caught the flicker of a wing in a tree nearby. I walked closer for a better look.

"What is it?" my cousin-sister asked, following me across the parking lot.

"A nuthatch," I said, pointing at the silhouette of the bird hopping vertically up and down the trunk of the tree.

"You really like birds, huh?" she laughed.

Any hope I had of being the cool older sister rapidly faded, but I shrugged with a smile. "Yeah."

"You're such a dork," she said.

I STARTED WATCHING birds, a single and solitary hobby, after I moved to Boston—in part, to escape the gray monotony of the city; in part, because my world was too loud. I'd found an old pair of Don's binoculars in one of my grandmother's suitcases, which I had packed and brought with me to Boston. I kneeled beside my window and watched the chickadees and nuthatches and sparrows that appeared. One year, a small flock of golden-crowned kinglets chose my backyard as a pit stop on their journey south. I walked cemeteries, which were some of the few green spaces in Boston, and ticked the pine siskin, the common nighthawk, and a few warblers and vireos off my life list.

* * *

AFTER WE LEFT the church, we drove down to Gallup to pick up one of my aunties, who had taken a Greyhound into town for my mother's memorial service. We stopped at a liquor store so they could stock up on booze. My aunt asked me if I wanted anything. I glanced at my cousin-sister and told them I didn't really drink.

But that night, while we prepared for the meal ahead, my aunties and I sat around the kitchen table and drank cheap vodka and smoked weed off a can of Bud Light. I could feel the smoke between my shoulder blades and in the tips of my fingers. My hands were clumsy and slow.

"Look at you," my auntie laughed, slapping my shoulder. "All buzzed."

I peeled carrots until my palms were orange. I picked a mountain of shells off the hard-boiled eggs. My mother's memorial service felt far away, as if there were no coming day—only each second, erased by the second after that. There was only the radio buzzing in the corner of my grandmother's kitchen. But as the smoke cleared, time as I had come to understand it collapsed, and I woke to the sound of my aunties crying and screaming at one another.

They're having completely different arguments, I thought. *No one can hear what anyone else is trying to say.* I left the kitchen table and walked down the hall and crawled into bed next to my cousin, who had long since fallen asleep.

THE NEXT MORNING, I woke to my aunt banging on our bedroom door. "I need *help*," she yelled.

I walked into the chaos of the kitchen, filled with mixing bowls and pots and pans, and walked out again. "I need a shower," I said, excusing myself. I ducked into the bathroom and stepped under the hot water and stared at the orange palms of my hands.

When I walked back into the kitchen, my aunt sent me across the street to beg folding chairs off Shorty. It had snowed overnight, and as I crossed the street, I admired the contrast between the white snow and red clay as I stained clean patches of snow with the mud on my shoes. Even the mud on the reservation was beautiful.

I returned with only a couple folding chairs. My cousin-sister sat at the table and mixed potato salad while my aunt complained about the roast—we had cooked it too long the night before, and it was too dry. Then she started complaining about the mud I tracked in on the floors.

I mopped both the living room and the kitchen, and when that was done, she made me practice reading my passage from the Old Testament while she diced another batch of hard-boiled eggs. She told me to look at the audience; to speak louder; to talk slower. I read and reread the passage until she was satisfied.

We walked into the church only a few minutes late.

The women in the front rows stood to greet us, and one by one, they embraced my aunt and whispered soft words into her hair. I hung back with my cousin-sister until my aunt pulled me forward. "This is Tweety's daughter," she announced.

They wrapped me in their arms and introduced themselves. I'm your grandma, your auntie, your cousin. I'm so sorry about your mom, they said.

The men—grandpas and uncles and cousins—remained seated and quiet.

The priest paced at the front of the church, hands clasped over his stomach, and asked if we were ready to begin. My aunt nodded, and he took his place behind the pulpit. "She was a sister, a mother, a grandmother," he recited. "A caregiver," he added from his notes.

He praised the gifts she had given to her family and friends in life—her love, her kindness, her generosity. He lamented the struggles she had surmounted, clichéd obstacles he rattled off the top of his head—nothing about life on the reservation, or alcohol, or abuse. He swiveled on his feet and left the pulpit, walking toward me. "I'm sure you thought you were an angel," he said, leaning down to thrust his smug face in mine.

I pulled away from him in surprise. He was trying to include me in her list of tribulations; in his grand narrative, I was an ungrateful, unruly child who offered little in exchange for my mother's love.

"You weren't an angel," he concluded, with conviction.

My lips parted, though I wasn't sure what I might say. My cousin-sister started giggling and then whispered something into her mother's ear.

"Stop it," my aunt scolded her, but my aunt was giggling, too.

I avoided looking at the priest again; I tried not to feed my growing anger. When I was called to the pulpit to read my passage, I could not find my voice. Despite all my aunt's coaching, I stumbled over each word.

ON THE FINAL morning I spent in my mother's hospital room, her pastor turned up at her door. "I came as soon as I heard," he said, assuming a position across from me at her bedside.

He was a short, mustachioed man who looked a little too clean, a little too put together, to be one of my mother's boyfriends. He wore his sunglasses around his neck on a black nylon strap. I didn't recognize him, and it was clear he didn't recognize me.

"I'm her daughter," I said. "Danielle."

"I'm so glad I came this morning," he exclaimed. "I'm so happy to meet you!" He looked like he might leap across the bed to give me a high five, but instead he folded his hands over his heart. "I've known your mother for a very long time. She's been coming to my church every Sunday for years. But you've never been?"

"I live in Boston," I said, shaking my head.

He nodded slowly, as if weighing his approach. "How is your mother doing?"

"She's dying," I said.

He looked into my eyes and said, with all sincerity, "I know if the Lord wanted to, he could raise Lee up out of this bed right now."

My mother's pastor was trying to instill false hope in me; he was trying to prolong my pain, not end it. Someone else might have latched on to his words, but I had little patience for and no trust in religious men. Silent, I stared at him until he finally looked down and away.

"Will you pray with me?" he asked, more humbly than I imagined he felt.

I ground my molars against the exposed gum at the back of my mouth, where my wisdom teeth should have been. I enjoyed the pinching feeling, like gravel against bare feet. "Sure," I said.

He placed his hand on my mother's forehead, which was beaded with condensation. He tried to balance himself on the bedrail with his right hand, but his stance was awkward, and the rail trembled under his weight as he spoke. "Dear Lord Jesus," he began, "if it is your will, please raise Lee out of this bed so that she might see her daughter here, with us on this day. And if it is not your will, if it is Lee's time, please take her into your hands." He paused and looked into my eyes. "We are all sinners," he said. "Even I, Lord, sin every day."

I refused to hold his gaze and instead focused on my mother's closed, swollen eyelids.

"If we accept you in our hearts, Lord, and ask forgiveness, we are forgiven, and we will be led into the gates of Heaven."

The longer he talked, the more angry I became. He convinced himself he was helping people like my mother—that he had shepherded them toward Heaven. But if all is forgiven by showing up to church every Sunday and muttering a few prayers, consequences become inconsequential. It didn't matter that my mother drank. It didn't matter that she had abandoned her children. She was forgiven; her sins were erased.[*]

---

[*] Bible study notes. April 11, 2008. " 'The vain regrets of yesterday / Have vanished through God's pardoning grace; / The guilty fear has passed away; / And joy has come to take its place.' CHRIST REMOVES OUR GUILTY PAST AND GIVES US A GLORIOUS FUTURE. And I am looking forward into Danielle Geller as a proud mom to have such a lovely daughter. You dear are my blessing in my heart."

I remained silent.

He cleared his throat. "We can do a memorial service for her, if you like. Will you be in town long?"

I shook my head and glanced at the clock on the far wall. "I'm leaving today."

"I see," he said. He wrote his name down in a notebook he carried, then tore out the page and passed it to me. He told me he would hold the service regardless and offered to record it for me. He could send the video and the few pictures he had of her if I liked.

"Okay," I said.

He took a few backward steps toward the door. "I'll let you have some alone time with your mom before you leave," he said, "but I really am glad to have met you, Darlene."

I smiled for the first time that morning. He hadn't even bothered to learn my name.

After my mother's pastor left her room, I stood there berating myself for agreeing to let him pray. If I were more like Eileen, I could channel my rage and do some real damage. I would be better equipped to stand up to men like him. But the longer I stood there, the more I realized I wasn't really angry at myself. I wasn't even angry at my mother. I was angry at things outside our control. I was angry at the broken communities we were born into, and the godly men who perpetuated the cycles of abuse. Who told us to seek happiness in ignorance and faith in a God who seemed indifferent to our suffering. Who taught us to forgive too readily, and that forgiveness restored power, when in my experience, forgiveness had only taken my power away.

AFTER THE SERVICE, our family returned to my grandmother's place. My grandmother's sisters—who I began to call my grandmothers, as everyone did—took their places in the kitchen—kneading flour and shortening into dough, which they worked with their light hands. They pulled the dough into round tortillas, and when the first tortilla came out of the cast-iron pan, my aunt nudged me toward the living room. "Help your sister start serving," she said.

We filled the plates with pot roast and potatoes and carrots and corn, egg salad and fruit salad and tortilla wedges. We carried the plates, one by one, to those seated around the folding tables in the living room.

I fixed myself one of the last plates and ate standing in the kitchen.

One of my grandmothers touched me lightly on the arm. "Your grandfather is going to say a few things," she said.

I followed her into the doorway. One of my grandfathers, tall and skinny as a cowboy, wearing boots and jeans and a worn button-down shirt, stood in the middle of the room. He bowed his head and stared at the floor. He spoke in Navajo, and no one translated his words. I closed my eyes and lowered my head and let the unfamiliar sounds wash over me. At one point, my grandmother rested her hand on my shoulder and whispered, "He's talking about you."

Then she passed a glass of water to my aunt, who carried it to my grandfather, who spoke a few more words and took a sip.

My grandmother nudged me forward. "Go."

My aunt took a sip from the same glass of water, then touched her fingers to her lips and her forehead.

When she passed the glass to me, I mimicked her performance, though its significance was lost. I passed the glass to one of my waiting grandmothers and fled to the corner of the room, too embarrassed to ask what had happened, or what was said, or what I was expected to do.

AFTER MY GRANDFATHER finished speaking and the family returned to their food, I retreated into the kitchen and began washing dishes. Another of my grandfathers walked into the kitchen and passed me a folded twenty-dollar bill. "For you," he said.

I thanked him and smiled, but neither of us knew what to say to the other next.

Before they left, my grandmothers gave me their email addresses and asked me to stay in touch. When they asked after my sister, I gave them the address for YCP and her inmate number; I told them she would love a letter and that I hoped they would write.

I VENTURED INTO my aunt's small backyard, ringed in by a chain-link fence, before the sun rose fully the next morning. The snow from the day before had already melted, and the red clay was dry and dusty again. As the sky shifted toward yellow and blue, I sat atop the weathered picnic table under the tall old tree and silently ate a bowl of Cap'n Crunch. My aunt's dog, Toro, settled on the bench by my side.

I watched a phainopepla, a sleek black bird, serenade the neighborhood from the top of a bush, just barely visible over the roof of my grandmother's house. I spied a kind of oriole, fluorescent orange, in a distant tree. A jay with a blue jacket and a gray belly perched on a branch above my head. I thumbed through the bird identification app on my phone: a western scrub jay, which inhabits the dry shrublands and pinyon and juniper forests of the West. Toro seemed unfazed by its loud, raspy call, but I apologized on our behalf. "I don't have any food for you," I said.

My aunt opened the back door and poked her head outside. "What are you doing out here?" she asked, surprising me.

My face burned red. "Just watching the birds," I said.

My aunt gasped loudly, and I quickly set my bowl of cereal down. I wasn't sure if I had done something wrong. But she ran past me and across the yard to a row of trash cans along the fence. "The stupid crows!" she yelled, gathering pieces of cardboard—the torn blue boxes from the Bud Light she'd bought in town—that had been strewn across the ground. She shoved the boxes, along with torn-open bags of food, back into the trash. "This is our personal business," she growled.

She disappeared into the house, then returned with a bottle of lighter fluid to set the can alight.

I tried not to laugh. I had forgotten and would not remember until much later that the reservation was dry, and that alcohol was not legal to buy or transport onto the Navajo Nation's land.

My aunt walked over and sat down next to me as the trash fire burned. "Do you pray?" she asked.

I shook my head.

"Let me teach you," she said. She stood up and gathered a pinch of dirt in her hand. "This should be corn pollen," she said, self-consciously. "But. You're supposed to pray, every morning at dawn. You pray to the four directions." And she closed her eyes and lifted her chin. "I walk with beauty before me," she prayed. "I walk with beauty behind me. I walk with beauty below me. I walk with beauty above me. I walk with beauty around me."

She motioned for me to stand, and she squared my shoulders toward the sun. "I walk in beauty," she coaxed me to say.

"I walk in beauty," I said, watching a cliff swallow swoop down to enter its nest, which it had built on the side of my grandmother's house. "I walk in beauty," I repeated, watching a cloud of bluebirds flit between the neighbor's bushes and the fence. "I walk in beauty," I repeated, reaching down to stroke Toro's head. "I walk in beauty," I repeated for the fourth time, listening to the phainopepla herald in the dawn.

them supposeable being

⤳✦⤳

GROWING UP, MY mother told us very little about her family. We didn't know our grandparents' names, or how many brothers and sisters she had. We weren't told when new cousins were born, or when her own parents and brother died.[*] After she met my father, my mother left her home and her mountains, her family and her future there. She once told me the only way to leave the reservation was to join the military or to marry off, and she told me never to go back.

The only things I knew about my family were the few things she told me when I visited her in South Florida. She told me that my grandfather was a medicine man and that her sister, my aunt, was a witch.

"She practices black magic," my mother said. Then she caught my eye and held my gaze, because I didn't dare look away. "But *we're* healers, baby. You have to use your magic for good."

If you are Diné, this next story is not, perhaps, a story you will want to read.

VISITING THE REZ felt eerily similar to visiting my mother in Florida. While my aunties and their friends partied, my cousins and I slumbered in front of the television and waited for the call that would jolt us awake—the call to pick them up, ferry them around, and feed and coax them into their beds at the end of the night.

[*] March 1, 1995. "I LOVE YOU" MOM. REMEMBER YOU STILL TOUCH MY HEART

One night, after we dropped off my aunt at her friend's, my cousins and I decided to drive down to Gallup to see a movie in the theater. We borrowed my aunt's truck; I offered to drive. The reservation glowed like the surface of the moon.

"I'm sorry about my mom," my cousin-brother said suddenly, but quietly.

"Don't be," I said. "My mom was the same way." I told him about the nights in Florida that I spent shuttling her back and forth between her house and Sneakers, her favorite dive bar.

"Yeah?" he asked.

"Yeah," I promised.

As we passed Sagebrush, the liquor store that sat just outside the border of the Navajo reservation, my cousin-sister popped her head out of the back seat and told her brother I didn't believe in skin-walkers. Her voice was laughing, incredulous.

I looked into the rearview mirror, into my cousin-sister's shining eyes, and then at her brother. "Do you?" I asked.

He seemed reluctant to speak. I knew very little about him, but I did know he had been living in Phoenix since he turned eighteen. And by virtue of his off-reservation-ness, I hated to admit, I trusted his opinion more than my cousin-sister's.

"I don't know," he said, sliding his palms over his thighs, "but I've seen some things."

"Like what?" I asked. I stared at the edge of the road and watched for rabbits, for coyotes—for what, I wasn't sure. The only animal I had seen on the reservation at night was a cow, a fat brown-and-white steer whose head hung stupidly into the road. But there was a chill in my blood—the same feeling I had when I was a girl sharing ghost stories in the darkness of a hurricane blackout.

"Like eyes," my cousin said. He was in the mountains at night with some friends when he heard a sound in the woods. Then he saw two red lights, like embers burning in the dark.

I told my cousins that *my* mother had told me *their* mother practiced black magic.

My cousin-sister laughed. "That's what my brother's ex-wife says. That's why he can't see his kids no more. She says we're all skin-walkers."

WHEN MY SISTER and I were little, we played a game we called "animals." We pretended to be horses and took turns vaulting over the ottoman on all fours, or we pretended to be lionesses and groomed our arms with our tongues. After *Jurassic Park* was released, the entire neighborhood played dinosaurs. The oldest boy claimed T. rex, and I became the queen of the raptors. Our youngest siblings were relegated to prey, the gazelle-necked Gallimimus of the open fields.

We stopped playing animals after we moved to Pennsylvania. We were too old, and the girls we met at school weren't interested in pretending to be horses and dinosaurs, though I still often crawled around the house on all fours.

In middle school, I told my best friend, Sherri, that my Indian grandmother had cursed me when I visited the reservation as a child. I told Sherri a wolf's spirit took over my body on full moons. All the wolf craved was flesh and blood.

I can't say Sherri believed me, but she certainly played along.

If I signaled the change with a growl, she would take off running. I followed her shrieks through the neighborhood, and she always ended up back at my apartment, where she yelled at Fran that I had tracked her home by the scent of her blood. Fran kept a giant stuffed banana plushie tucked behind the TV hutch, and she would whack both Sherri and me with the banana until I, laughing hysterically, changed back into the girl I had always been.

I did not realize what I was claiming to be, or why it might be taboo.

YOU AREN'T SUPPOSED to talk about skin-walkers. Stories inspire fear, and fear makes them stronger. Fear draws them to you, like blood draws sharks in the water.

Still, the stories are told. In Diné Bizaad, a skin-walker is yee naaldlooshii—"with it, he goes on all fours." In some stories, skin-walkers are described as animals, coyotes, wolves, or owls, with evil red or yellow eyes. In others, skin-walkers are half-animal, half-human, adorned with antlers or skulls or animal pelts. Skin-walkers acquire their powers of transformation through black magic; through the most evil of deeds. And though they can use their magic to cause harm, most of the stories about skin-walkers that persist in legend sound like hauntings: A skin-walker dashes in front of a car's headlights, or taps on the window of a moving car, or climbs onto the roof of a home.

The accounts of skin-walkers vary, but in the stories I read and am told, one thing remains constant: During the day, yee naaldlooshii walks around in human skin.

THERE ARE TWO stories about the way Pauline Tom, my great-grandmother, died.*

The way my aunt tells it, Pauline Tom fell at night in her own backyard. She froze to death in the middle of winter because she could not crawl home, and no one heard her cries.

The way one of my grandmothers tells it, Pauline Tom's injuries were not sustained from tripping and falling. When the coroner examined her body, he said the injuries she sustained made it look like she had been dropped from a great height. "There are things out here," my grandmother said. "Evil things." Things not easily explained.

I ALWAYS CONSIDERED my mother superstitious. She told me it was bad luck to wear a ring on any finger but your ring finger. She told me that if you saw an owl during the day, someone close to you

---

* Three; Bible study notebook, March 20, 2008: "Grandma Pauline you now with God and the rest of our family. You are no longer suffering." And from March 22, 2008. "I started this day with the fact that I lost my best friend Pauline Tom my grandma."

would die. She told me not to keep the image of a wolf in my house, because it would bring bad luck. She told me to never stare at the moon.

My cousin-sister and I visited the Navajo Nation's zoo, and I was surprised to find a pair of great horned owls perching on an old tree in broad daylight. According to the placard in front of their exhibit, they had been injured on the road and rehabilitated by the zoo.

When I told my cousin-sister what my mother had told me about owls, she laughed. "I never heard that before."

My aunt held an entirely different set of superstitions. She told me if you didn't eat spicy food, it meant you were a jealous person. She told me to never buy an animal or I would become poor.

I could not make myself believe in the superstitions my mother held.

I could not make myself believe in yee naaldlooshii.

My aunt and my mother stopped speaking before my mother died, I believed, not because my aunt practiced black magic but because they disagreed about how to care for their families best.

My family is not full of skin-walkers. It feels more complicated than that.

But one night, my cousin-sister and I woke up to the sound of something scrabbling on the roof. She reached for my arm under the blanket.

"It's probably a raccoon," I whispered.

"How did it get up there?" she whispered back.

I imagined a friendly masked face with bright eyes and fuzzy ears; I imagined turning on the light and making us safe. Then I remembered a story my aunt had told us of a tall figure she saw through the window at night, and I could not make myself get out of bed.

[Exhaustion]

꘏꘏꘏✦꘏꘏꘏

IN TOTAL, I spent only six days on the reservation for my mother's memorial service. The days felt much longer. I had begun to feel like a small, nervous dog, always ready to bolt out of danger, but also, always longing to please.

My aunt drank more than I expected, and each time she opened a beer, she said it was an exception, as if looking for absolution. *Of course, Auntie. Have another. Let me join you.* But after the carrots, I did not drink again.

My aunt didn't seem to want to talk about my mother. She stopped sharing stories with me. After the memorial service, she lost momentum, and she spent long hours sitting in the kitchen alone, with tears leaking constantly down her face.

One night, one of my aunt's neighbors and her nephew came over to visit. The nephew was twenty-something years old, around my age, and visiting from Portland, and our aunties seemed to want to hook us up. They cajoled us into taking a photo together, and before she snapped the picture, my aunt pulled my hoodie down to expose my bare shoulder. "Show a little skin!" she laughed.

After they left, my aunt passed out in her room, and my cousin-brother and I staked out opposite couches. He turned on the television, but neither of us watched what was on. We were too preoccupied with our phones.

Portland asked me for my number, and my aunt pressured me to give it to him, though he wasn't quite my type. He was a little too skinny, a little too feminine, and a little too cool for me. I gave him my number because I was lonely, even surrounded by my family, and I wondered what he thought about returning to the reservation after living so many years away.

He sent me a message, asking me what I was doing.

Just watching TV, I told him, then added, *If you want to come over, we could hang out for a little while.*

Are you drinking?

Not tonight, I said. I told him I was the DD, in case someone needed a ride.

Well, he said, *it's late. I don't think you have to drive now.*

I set my phone on the coffee table and chewed on the edge of my nail. I knew I should just go to bed. I watched my cousin-brother stand and walk out the front door. I lay down and pulled one of my aunt's heavy blankets over me and stared at the television, though my eyelids started to droop. I picked up my phone and sent him another text, telling him we could do something the next day.

My phone dinged. *We're on our way!* he wrote. *My aunt wants to hang.*

I panicked. *My aunt is asleep,* I told him, but he didn't respond again.

I jumped off the couch and ran outside, but I stopped short when I saw my cousin-brother standing at the corner of the house beside two tall figures. The red end of his cigarette flared in the dark.

I walked slowly toward them, and he introduced me as his cousin to two of his friends. They said quiet hellos.

"That guy from Portland is on his way over," I said, nervously. "I told him everyone's asleep—"

My cousin-brother sighed and, shaking his head, turned away from me.

A car pulled up in front of the house. I walked down the driveway to meet them. Portland's aunt barreled out the passenger-side door with her little son balanced on one hip, two bottles of beer held in her other hand.

"My aunt's asleep," I told her. "I don't think you should come in."

"I have my son with me," she yelled. "Where am I going to take him?" Then she pushed past me toward the house.

"Sorry," Portland said, walking around the front of the car. "She got in a fight with Gramps."

We walked slowly up the driveway, past my cousin-brother and his friends, and back inside. His aunt sat on the sofa, the hem of her T-shirt tucked under her chin. Her son clung to her breast and nursed as she tipped a beer toward her mouth. She told us to sit by the fire.

I led him across the living room and into the old garage, which was more of a storage room and separated by only a curtain, bundled to one side. We sat beside the wood-burning stove, though the fire had already burned down.

"So, you're from Boston," he said. His eyes wandered, drunk-lost.

"Yeah," I said. "I'm just visiting for my mom's memorial."

He tilted his head to the side. "I'm sorry."

"Oh my god," his aunt complained loudly from the couch. "You two are so boring. Give me something to watch."

Taking her cue, he leaned in to kiss me. He smelled like cheap beer, but his hands were gentle on my face. I returned the kiss, a peck on his bottom lip, but turned my head away.

"My family is trying to convince me to move here," I said, trying to change the subject. It was a fleeting comment my aunties and grandmothers had been making throughout my visit—after the memorial service, one of my grandmothers had told me about an opening at her school's library and had given me her work email to send her my résumé.

"I wouldn't if I were you," he laughed. "But look where I am now."

The little boy suddenly appeared at my side; his hands stretched toward the stove. I grabbed him and pulled him into my lap. I thought he might act as a barrier between me and Portland, but even with the boy in my lap, Portland ducked his head in to steal kisses on my lips and my cheeks and my forehead.

"It's crazy," he whispered near my ear, "that the two of us would meet here like this."

I stayed quiet. He was looking for a love story, and I was looking for something else. Something I couldn't quite figure out, myself.

A door opened, and my aunt stumbled out of her bedroom. "What are you doing here?" she yelled when she saw her neighbor on the couch.

"My nephew!" she yelled back, motioning toward the two of us.

I shifted her son out of my lap and stood up. I wanted to apologize to my aunt, but I didn't know how.

My aunt groaned, "Oh, fine," then disappeared into the kitchen. Everyone seemed onboard with a love story but me. She returned with a can of beer and dropped onto the couch.

I fled the garage and tried to hide in the kitchen, but Portland followed me. I leaned against the kitchen counter, and he rested his hands on my hips. I pressed my palm into his chest and guided him into a chair and angled my own to face him, but at my own safe distance.

He leaned back and regarded me with eyes dark and serious. "You have a boyfriend, don't you?" he asked.

"Yes," I sighed, relieved.

"Then why?"

"I don't know," I said. "It's complicated."

He glanced around the kitchen and rocked his head side to side. "You have the cutest smile," he said, finally.

My shoulders fell. It would be easy to fuck him, but I worried what my cousin-sister would think. Tomorrow, having fucked him wouldn't be enough.

He stretched out his hands and lifted me into his lap. He slid his hands down the front of my jeans, but I grabbed his wrists and pinned them in place.

"I need to sleep," I said, standing and backing away slowly.

"Come home with me," he begged.

I shook my head and walked out of the kitchen and down the hall to my cousin-sister's room. Portland followed. I held my hand on her doorknob, and he leaned down to kiss my neck. It was like I lived in two bodies: one, pushing him toward the living room; the other, dragging him into me. I tilted my head and whispered into his ear, "Tomorrow."

He leaned back and smiled, "Okay."

I ducked into my cousin-sister's room and changed into my sleeping shirt in the dark. As I slid under the blankets beside her, she giggled, "Did he just walk you to my door?"

"Yeah," I laughed, both nervous and surprised that she was still awake.

"What a dork," she sighed sleepily.

I lay there in the dark, my eyes wide, and listened for the sound of her soft sleep breaths. *If it weren't for my cousin-sister,* I thought, *I would be with him.* But I was trying to teach us another way.

LATE THE NEXT afternoon, my cousin-sister and I hiked to the top of Window Rock. Patches of snow still sheltered in the shadow of juniper and rock at the higher elevation. My cousin-sister, younger and fitter, scampered ahead. We reached the top of the sandstone cliffs as the sun began setting over the land, pale yellow in its winter dress.

I told my cousin-sister I would miss her. We promised to stay in touch.

Shorty gave me a ride back to the airport the next day, and both my aunt and my cousin-sister tagged along. The drive was strangely quiet. At the gate, we parted with dry eyes and reserved hugs.

In Boston, Marc met me at the gate. He carried my bag to the car. On the drive home, he rested his hand on my knee and asked me how my trip had gone.

I stared out the window at the thousand city lights. "It was pretty much what I expected," I said, avoiding too many details. "It felt like home."

The Art of Living Dangerously

MY SISTER WAS paroled early for good behavior. She gave her parole officer the address for my father's motel. I didn't think it was a good idea, but no one asked me what I thought. Two days after her release, they called me—both loud and angry-drunk.

"She told me it was okay to have a beer," my father said.

In the background, I heard my sister yell that she hadn't said that at all.

While I sat on the phone, they argued about who was the bigger hypocrite—my sister for having a beer while on parole, or my father for drinking an entire bottle of bourbon in front of her.

"It doesn't matter," I kept saying. "It doesn't matter. You both need to stay sober while she's there."

He called me three times after I hung up the phone, and when I didn't respond, he sent a series of texts:

Your sister left.

Blame me so be it.

PS. Your sister is a worthless bitch.

Call me after I'm dead.

See you in the next life.

Love Daddy.

I didn't hear from my sister until the next morning, when she called me from a number I didn't recognize. Over the line, I could hear the steady purr of tires against asphalt and a hollow rush of air. She was in a car, heading to Pittsburgh. I worried what her parole officer would say when they found out she was gone.

"He told me I wasn't worthy of a son like Sebastian," Eileen said.

"He was drunk," I said, trying to excuse him; to diminish him; to help her believe that what our father said wasn't true.

But Eileen wasn't listening, not really. "I don't think Sebastian even needs me, Danielle," she said, casually. "He's not like other kids."

"I don't think you need to worry about him right now," I said. I felt guilty even saying the words—knowing my grandmother and my father wanted me to convince her to be a better mother, to find a job, to settle down. They wanted her to accept responsibility and build a home for her son. But that life felt too far away. "You need to worry about staying clean. Just focus on that, okay?"

She made a noncommittal sound.

I told her to call me later. To come see me in Boston. I told her I could help.

IN JULY, EILEEN hopped on a freight train from Pittsburgh to New York, then bought a bus ticket to Boston. She caught the last train from the station and landed on my couch near two in the morning. I made her a bowl of ramen noodles and brought it to her in the living room. She pulled a package of onion-and-chive crackers out of her pack and crushed them over the top.

I sat on the opposite end of the couch and watched her eat.

"How long do you plan on staying?" I asked.

"I don't know," she said. "Some of my friends here are heading up to Vermont. I've never been up there, but I was thinking of going with them."

"It's pretty," I said, remembering a long weekend Marc and I had spent there with Marie, who had moved there with her boyfriend to help him clear out an old family house. We picked black raspberries out of their garden. Went swimming in a bone-cold creek, where I met my first American dipper, a stocky gray bird twerking on the bank.

"Some of my friends want me to do the sugar beet harvest this winter," she said.

I laughed. "You didn't last two weeks on the fruit farm when you were a kid."

She said nothing. She shrugged one shoulder and ate quickly and avoided my eyes.

I told her I needed sleep but offered to make breakfast in the morning.

She said okay.

I stood and walked to the stairs. I glanced back at my sister, lying on the couch and typing furiously on her phone. I couldn't imagine this was a scene that would last.

The next morning, I tried making Eileen's eggs the way she liked them—yolks runny and warm—but I overcooked them. The yolks were too firm when I flipped them out of the pan.

"People out West don't know what dippy eggs are," Eileen laughed, eating without complaint. "I asked for a dippy egg in a diner and the waitress looked at me like I was nuts."

After breakfast, I carried our mother's box downstairs. I lifted the lid off the box and pulled out a manila envelope of letters Eileen had written to our mother. I handed her one that she had written to our mother after she visited us in middle school. "I hope you still love me," Eileen read aloud. "If you move up here it would be great. I could see my sister and you. You wouldn't need a guy . . . if you would move up here I could visit you and sleep there and have fun and at Halloween you could dress me up like you used to."

Eileen laughed bitterly and wiped the tears from her eyes. "I remember writing that—but I remembered it being a lot angrier."

I handed her a stack of our mother's diaries, and she flipped through the pages, skimming lines quickly, but she looked disappointed. I couldn't tell if her impatience was simply withdrawal, the absence of her name in our mother's handwriting, or both. We talked little as she read, but when she slid the last diary back into its box, she sighed. "She doesn't say anything important."

"What do you mean?" I asked, though I knew what she meant.

I had felt the same disappointment reading our mother's diaries, filled with tallies of money owed, men kissed, meals prepared, houses cleaned. I had hoped to find more heartfelt expressions of our mother's regrets—some accounting of the daughters she left, but I was forced to look for those sentiments between the written lines. I hoped Eileen would elaborate, or give voice to similar thoughts, but my sister shrugged and rubbed her hands over her face.

"I'm feeling dope sick," she said, ending the conversation.

My sister was using again.

I took Eileen up to my room and turned off the window AC and wrapped her in blankets, despite Boston's summer heat, because she said she was cold. I gave her my laptop to watch Netflix. On my desktop, I distracted myself researching rehabs and detox centers in the city to call the next day.

EILEEN FOUND A bed at a detox in Roxbury. She called me at work to tell me she would be in for six days and apologized for missing my birthday. Then she asked me to bring her a pair of pajamas and a pack of cigarettes. On my way home from work, I stopped at a Goodwill and bought her a pair of soft gray jersey pants.

Two days later, she left the detox center early with a kid she met there. They showed up at my apartment together, high.

"They had fucking bedbugs," Eileen complained as she walked up the stairs, and in the light of the kitchen, she lifted her shirt to show me the raised red marks on her side.

She dragged her pack into the middle of the kitchen floor and began folding things into each of its pockets—her clothes, her map, her phone charger.

"You're leaving?" I asked.

"Yeah. I mean, I feel like I'm in your way." She was jumpy. Edgy. Her words drifted into one another.

"Eileen, all my roommates moved out. I'm basically living here alone with Marc. You aren't in my way."

"I just feel like you don't want me here," she insisted, disappearing into the living room.

"I think you should stay," her friend chimed in. "If you want to get clean, Boston is the place to be."

As if on cue, Eileen poked her head into the kitchen and waved a plastic package with a bright orange label in the air. "They did give us Narcan," she laughed. "Other places don't do that."

I crossed my arms over my chest and drifted down the hall.

"Are you worried, Danielle?" she asked. She tried to focus her eyes on mine but they wandered, lost. "Are you mad?"

I was too angry, too frustrated, for words. I shook my head.

"Are you worried I'll overdose?"

"I'm not worried you'll overdose," I sighed. I didn't believe she *could* overdose—as if the amount of time she had been shooting heroin had inoculated her, somehow. "I just thought we would spend some time together. I thought we would talk."

She rolled her eyes. "What are we going to talk about?"

"Everything? You said in your letters to me, over and over, that there are things you want to talk about. You can't keep running away."

"I'm not good at these things," she laughed, circling the kitchen. "You know that."

I told her I had a headache and that I was going to bed, but she followed me upstairs and sat on the corner of my bed. "Come here, Danielle," she said, gentle and quiet. She opened her arms, and I relaxed into her hug. "You know I love you, right?" she said.

I told her I loved her, too.

"Are you scared I'm going to overdose?" she asked again.

I covered my face with my hands. "It's not as simple as that. Can't you see? Everything keeps repeating. All of this has happened before. I don't want you to end up like our parents."

Eileen took my hands, drew them down into her lap, and looked into my eyes. "I'm just happy you made it out," she said, softly. "It had to get one of us, you know?"

* * *

"have you heard from your sister?" Marc asked me, two days later, as we browsed gaming keyboards at a computer center. He wanted to buy me a new mechanical keyboard for my birthday because the keyboard that had come with my desktop was old, the letters worn off the surface of the keys. I didn't need to look at the keys to type, but he swore mechanical keyboards were better.

I told him I hadn't heard from Eileen, but minutes later, she called me as we walked out of the store and toward the car. She was sobbing so hard I couldn't figure out what she was trying to say. I kept asking her what was wrong, if she was okay, but it seemed like she couldn't stop crying.

"I don't know where I am," she said, finally. "I'm scared."

I asked her to describe her surroundings. She told me she was by the police station, by the woods. I asked her what police station, what woods, but she just kept repeating those two words.

"Can you go to the police station? Can you ask someone where you are?"

"No, Danielle!" she yelled. "They're just going to arrest me. People keep. People keep walking away from me."

"Can you just go ask them where you are?" I begged.

She screamed no, no, no. "You don't even care," she sobbed, and then she hung up the phone.

I pulled up the map on my phone and thumbed around the eight police stations pinged in downtown Boston. The police station, the woods. I wondered if she might still be in Roxbury, near where the treatment center had been. "Head toward the Fens," I told Marc.

I tried calling Eileen back, but she wouldn't answer. *I'm trying to find you,* I sent her by text.

When she finally answered, I could hear a man's voice in the background.

"Who is that?" I asked. "Can you put him on?"

"Yeah," she sighed. She told the man I was her sister as she passed him the phone.

He told me she was near the police headquarters on Tremont Street. We were heading the right way.

"I'll be there soon," I told him. "Can you stay with her?"

"How long you gonna be?" he asked.

"Ten minutes," I promised, hanging up.

My sister was sitting in the parking lot across from the station when we arrived. "Can I see your glasses?" she asked as I approached.

"Why?"

"Because I want to fucking see where I am," she yelled.

Reluctantly, I handed her my glasses, and she walked quickly toward a fenced-in wooded lot. The man I'd spoken to on the phone was still there, and he walked toward me. He wore a jacket over blue scrubs. "I tried to convince her to go to the clinic," he said, pointing to a building nearby. "At least to get a drink of water."

I nodded, staring after her. "Did she say what happened?"

"She said she lost her glasses," he said. "I walked back there to try to find them—but, you know, it's scary back there."

I wrapped my arms around my stomach. "I think she was drugged," I said quietly.

"You should get her checked out," he said. "I can go in and give them a heads-up. They even have an NA meeting going on right now."

I thanked him, but I couldn't see Eileen anymore, and I was worried. I walked toward the woods and started calling her name. To my relief, she answered, and I begged her to come back to me.

She walked out of the woods and handed me my glasses, but she refused to go to the clinic. "They're going to admit me," she said, her voice again breaking into a sob.

"They won't," I promised. "Please. Just do it for me."

I picked up her pack and led her inside, and they rushed us through urgent care. But in the room she only cried. "I want to go home," she repeated. "What are these people going to do? Nothing. Nothing. Nothing."

The doctor told me he couldn't treat her; they didn't have the resources. He told me I should take her to the ER.

"I'm not going to the fucking ER," Eileen yelled, jumping off the examination table and stalking out of the room.

My heart sank. I knew I would never get her there. "Thank you," I said, turning to go.

The doctor reached out to me and wrapped her arm around my shoulders. "Is there anyone else with you?" she asked.

I thought of Marc but shook my head. He wouldn't know what to do with Eileen.

"No family?"

I shook my head again. "Our mom died last year," I said. The doctor sighed and hugged me tighter.

"Take care of yourself," she said. "Come back to see us. We have counselors and support groups for families."

I thanked her but quickly followed Eileen outside.

The entire drive home, she kept asking for my glasses, to look for the guy who had stolen her phone, her glasses, and some jewelry out of her pack before she had regained consciousness. "I'm going to beat the shit out of him," she insisted. At an intersection where they had hung out, she leapt out of the car. I tried to grab her pack by its straps, but she beat my arm with her fists until I let go.

The light turned green, and Marc drove on, but I asked him to go back.

Whoever had stolen Eileen's things wasn't there. We found her at a bus stop down the block. She was talking to two crusty-looking punks, smoking under the glass shelter. Marc pulled over to the curb and I rolled down the window and asked her, again, to let me take her to the ER.

"You can take *me* to the ER," a woman sitting on the bench said. She looked homeless.

The two punks laughed.

Neither of them knew anything about the guy Eileen was looking for. She got into the car after I finally agreed to just take her home. She collapsed on the couch, and I brought her a handful of ibuprofens and a glass of water. I turned out the lights and walked upstairs.

In the middle of the night, a loud crash made me jump out of bed. I raced downstairs, worried my sister had tried to get up and tripped over something, or down the stairs. But my sister was still on the couch.

"The ceiling is falling," she said quietly.

I turned on the light to find her covered in white dust and broken ceiling tiles. One of my old roommates had tried to hang a lamp from the tiles without securing it properly, and they had been sagging for months, threatening to fall.

"Are you okay?" I asked.

She nodded but didn't open her eyes.

I picked the tiles off of her and stacked them against the wall. I sat on the edge of the coffee table and brushed the dust off her arms. "Are you sure you don't need to go to the hospital?" I asked.

"I'm fine," she groaned, shifting slightly on the couch. She didn't even have the energy to turn over. "I think I overdosed. I think they gave me Narcan."

I couldn't say anything. I could only stare at her. I felt naïve, stupid, for believing she would stay safe. That she wouldn't die. Gently, I shook her shoulder and asked again if I could take her to the ER.

"I'm fine," she repeated. "It's happened before." She draped one arm over her eyes and mumbled, "Can you get me a trash can?"

I brought her the white can from the bathroom and set it beside the couch. She smelled like a nursing home. I sat on the coffee table next to her and watched her chest rise and fall. When it seemed like she was deep in sleep, I walked upstairs to bed.

The next morning, she and her pack were gone. She texted me from the train yard to say she was leaving again.

knowing it was just another one of his lies

MY FATHER LOST his job, and then he lost his room at the motel, and then Marc agreed to let my father come stay with us in Boston for a while. He arrived on my porch in the early morning—his face thinner, his clothes hanging loosely off his frame. He carried a duffel bag in each hand, one packed with clothing, his reading glasses, and his netbook, and the other with two pounds of loose tobacco and a U.S. postal scale. He'd packed envelopes filled with tobacco seeds, which he harvested from the plant that grew on my grandmother's windowsill. He planned to sell the seeds on eBay, along with two copper hammers he'd milled at his last job.

He apologized for waking me up.

I could smell the sour hint of alcohol on his breath, but I bit my tongue. *I'll take care of him,* my mother had said so candidly, as if we were talking about the family dog.

While Marc and I worked, my father spent hours riding the Red Line train between Ashmont and South Station; he collected cans out of the trash to return for their five-cent deposits. And on the trash days in my neighborhood, he combed the streets for discarded treasures that he brought home and proudly showed me: a pair of barely worn slippers, ten yards of fabric, a functional DVD player, a wooden wine rack, a Pyrex pie dish. He gave me first dibs, and I kept the dish.

It reminded me of the years in Florida my father spent junking, hauling broken electronics and appliances out of the garbage to fix and sell at the flea market. He'd had all the collection days memorized for the wealthiest neighborhoods. Sometimes, Grandma let us go junking with him and Fran. We left before sunrise. At the convenience store, he bought us bottles of Yoo-hoo and bags of Fritos, and then my sister and I played lookout, hawkeyed, watching for the familiar glint of crystal or milk glass. On one lucky day, I found a bootlegged copy of the *Animal House* soundtrack, which became my favorite cassette tape. I spent months crooning the songs around the house.

Sometimes Grandma let us go with him to the flea market, held in the parking lot of an old drive-in movie theater. The curving white screen sheltered the market from the sun through the early afternoon. We helped our father arrange his wares on fold-up tables, then wandered the market ourselves. The other vendors gave us Hershey's kisses and M&Ms, and he bought us hot dogs and cheesy fries and soft pretzels from the concession stand.

Those fleeting moments, we felt like family.

On my way home from work one day, I spied two cords dangling over the lip of one of my neighbor's garbage cans. I lifted the lid off the top and pulled two printer cables out of a broken wicker basket. *He could sell these*, I thought, tucking them inside my purse.

When he collected enough junk, we loaded his treasures into my granny cart, the one I used for groceries, and we wheeled them down to the neighborhood secondhand store. The store was piled wall to wall with junk, and only a narrow aisle down the center of the store was open to customers, so we had to walk single file through the store.

"We got some good junk," my father said, approaching the counter, and he started pulling things out for display. The owner dug through the top layer and reached into his pocket as if to make an offer, but then he reconsidered and shook his head. "I just got the second notice on my rent," he said. "I can't afford to buy anything."

My father complained the whole way home. The owner of the thrift store didn't know what he was doing; he didn't understand the value of the things my father had found. "I could make him a lot of money," my father said, "if he just cleared the real junk out of there."

"Maybe you could ask if he wants a partner," I said.

He paused as we passed a municipal trash can and dug out two aluminum cans. "Maybe I'll open my own thrift store."

But he didn't. He wouldn't. He started spending more and more time away from the apartment.

Some nights, when he was too drunk to come home, he slept under a bridge downtown.

One morning, he staggered home with a fresh black eye and someone else's baggy tank top. "It was his favorite shirt," he mumbled when I pressed him.

"What are you talking about?"

He told me a kid on Spice had punched him, then felt guilty and had given my father the shirt off his back.

My father created an OkCupid profile, and he met a hypochondriac who lived in Vermont. He told me he would be going to stay with her for a while, to look for love. A few weeks later, she bought a pair of cheap rings and told him they were going to get married. My grandmother bought them a car. But their relationship didn't last. He put salt in the eggs and brewed the coffee too strong, and soon he was back with me again.

He nested in the spare room. He found a set of shelves on the street and filled them with shipping materials and for his eBay business. We brought one of my old roommate's computer desks into the room so he could work on his Android apps.

One night after my father passed out, Marc cornered me in the kitchen. "What's the plan?" he asked. He had become impatient with my father's constant coming and going; impatient with the nights he came home drunk.

"What do you mean?" I asked, avoiding his eyes.

"We need a plan. How long is he staying this time?"

"I don't know," I said. "It doesn't work that way."

He touched my arm. I felt myself recoil but tried to hold still.

"We could be happy," he said.

I said nothing; I walked upstairs. I wasn't convinced we could be happy. I wasn't convinced I would ever find a way out from under my father; if I would ever find my way to air.

"I MISS FRAN," my father confessed one day, a gentle buzz shining in his eyes. It was clear from the way he always talked that Fran had been the love of his life.

"I do, too," I told him.

"You know she was a fucking cokehead," he said, his voice twisting suddenly with an accusing, vindictive edge.

I nodded, but I hadn't known. He seemed hurt—as if I had been willing to overlook her addictions but not his. But looking inward, I knew that if I had met Fran as an adult, I might not have loved her the way I had loved her then.

THAT FALL, WITHOUT telling Marc, I applied for an MFA program at the University of Arizona. The program was reputable, fully funded, and both close enough to and far enough away from my mother's family. With my application I submitted some of the early pages I had written about my mother.

The program accepted me in the spring. I surprised Marc with the news and tried to make it sound like a fun adventure, though he could tell I was leaving with or without him. We made tentative plans to move to Tucson together, but then his boss offered him a position outside Philly. He said he could move to Tucson a year later, after he got more experience under his belt. When he told me he was moving to Pennsylvania, I realized I would have to move with him, because I could not afford to stay in Boston alone. I sobbed uncontrollably for days.

We moved temporarily into a senior-living community, like my grandmother's, where he worked as a network administrator. I didn't bother finding a job. Instead, I lay on the couch and eavesdropped on the neighbors—an elderly man who played the piano and a woman who yelled at her cat. I stopped showering. I read obsessively and spent all day building messy metropolises in *Cities: Skylines*.

A FEW WEEKS before I moved to Tucson, I borrowed Marc's car to visit Eileen in Pittsburgh. I brought her one of the bonsai saplings— a little cocktail stick of a black pine—that Marc and I had started from seed in our crisper drawer.

The night I arrived, Eileen made chicken and dumplings in her slow cooker, and we ate while watching *RuPaul's Drag Race* on her couch.

We painted an accent panel on one of the walls in her living room a shade of blue-gray.

We visited the National Aviary and wandered slowly through each habitat—the wetlands and its pink spoonbills, the grasslands and its sparrows. We passed a pair of roadrunners anxiously pacing the perimeters of their glassed-in enclosure and made disapproving sounds. We entered the rain forest exhibit during a feeding, and an employee gave us a few dried mealworms, which we held in the palms of our hands. I raised my hand over my head, and a golden-breasted starling—emerald headed, cobalt backed, with a long, scis-soring tail—landed on my pinky, and another on my finger, to snap the worms off my palm. Eileen stood beside me, arm outstretched, but the birds visited every hand but hers. Laughing, she dumped the mealworms over the rail.

We walked along the Allegheny River one evening and watched a small flock of tubby cedar waxwings hunt insects over the river.

We ordered rum and cokes at Eileen's favorite rooftop bar, and the alcohol dislodged something in our throats. Later, we lay side by side in her bed and whispered secrets at the ceiling in the dark. We felt closer than we had ever been.

Her boyfriend, a man in his middle age, took us to see *Inside Out*. They both ordered drinks at the bar. My sister and I were the loud-est in the theater—laughing and crying by turns. After the movie, from my place in the back seat of his car, I watched their hands—interlaced, thumbs stroking the backs of each other's hands.

Every morning, I drove her to the methadone clinic; she was trying to get clean again. I waited in the car.

One morning I watched her sleep, flat on her stomach—her shoulders warming in the sun. I stared at the tattoo, two twined feathers on her shoulder blade, that she had gotten as a teenager after a fight we had. A bead pinched the end of each feather, and our initials were inscribed on the beads.

The last morning of my visit, we sat beside her garden, a small tilled patch behind her apartment building. She knelt in the grass to idle-pull weeds. "I want to live," she said, sounding optimistic about her recovery. "I want to know what my tomatoes taste like." A chirping cardinal hopped from branch to branch above her head.

I RETURNED TO Philly to find two bags of garbage leaning against the counter in the kitchen. They hadn't moved since before I left. I picked up a sock in the living room and found three brown casings, like thick grains of wild rice, on the floor. I scooped them into a glass jar to see what might grow. Days later, the apartment was full of them—beautiful bottle-green blowflies with little white feet. They buzzed inside the curtains and butted their heads against the windows, full of light.

We took the screens out of the windows and tried to flush them out of the apartment, but each morning, a new crop emerged. I spent hours crawling around the living room to hunt the young—hardened pupal casings sheathed between carpet fibers and protected by the shade of sofa, chair, and lamp—and the recently hatched, with soft wings and gray bodies, that clung to the baseboards and cabinet doors. I crushed them between my fingers before they gained flight.

TITLE: "Tweety" Lee holds Danielle in front of the state-line sign for Arkansas.

DATE: 1988

TYPE OF RESOURCE: color photographs

DESCRIPTION: My mother holds me in front of the Arkansas state sign. The photograph is blurry, our faces indistinct. On the back, in blue pen, she has written, "Going to Arizona when Danielle was 2 years old." It is one of the only photographs from that trip.

TITLE: "Tweety" Lee grills meat and green chilis on the Navajo reservation.

DATE: undated

TYPE OF RESOURCE: color photographs

DESCRIPTION: My mother stands in front of a grill loaded with meat and green chilis. She holds a cooking utensil in one hand and a beer in the other. Her face is obscured by a puff of smoke. By the earth, the trees, and the chaha'oh—a weathered, cedar shade—in the background, I can tell this is the reservation. I do not recognize the place.

TITLE: Eckerd index print 000102.

DATE: 2002 December 17

TYPE OF RESOURCE: color photographs

DESCRIPTION: An index print for film from a disposable camera developed by Eckerd Pharmacy. The photographs were taken during one of my mother's visits to the Navajo reservation, though none of the photographs are labeled with names or places.

TITLE: Woman in white jacket sits above corral in twilight.

DATE: 2002 December 17

TYPE OF RESOURCE: color photographs

DESCRIPTION: A photograph taken by my mother during one of her visits to the Navajo reservation. An unknown woman in a white jacket sits above a corral. The sky is blue-clouds as the sun begins to set.

TITLE: Draft of a letter to one of "Tweety" Lee's cousins.

DATE: 1996 August 27

TYPE OF RESOURCE: personal correspondence

DESCRIPTION: A draft of a letter my mother sent to one of her cousins following the news of her father's illness and her sister's desire to remove him from life support. On the previous page, she writes, "I felt so upset to the point where I might just get trashed just to sleep and not think of how mad she has done such a thing . . ." On this, the second page, she continues, "You know I know he can live more years if we all take-care of him, this means all his medicine-man prays and when he's with me eating good meals and him just being around he will make me happy." My grandfather died four years later, on July 26, 2000, though he never joined my mother in South Florida.

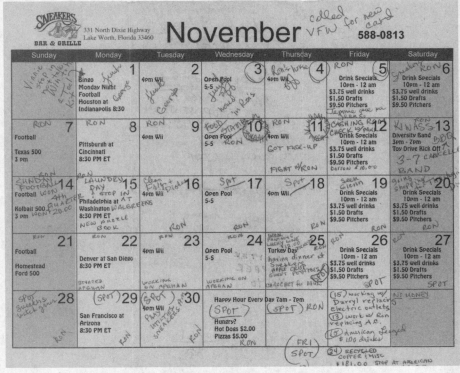

TITLE: November social calendar for Sneakers Bar & Grille.

DATE: 2010

TYPE OF RESOURCE: (printed matter)

DESCRIPTION: If my mother kept a diary in 2010, she did not store it with the rest. The only account of her days is a salmon-colored flier, a social calendar for the month of November at Sneakers Bar & Grille. She tracks her spotting period and the days she spent with her then ex-husband Ron. She begins a new puzzle book on the fifteenth. She shops for Thanksgiving dinner on the twentieth but also celebrates "Turkey Day" at Sneakers with apple crisp and sweet potatoes. She works on a crocheted afghan for a man named Paul.

IV

What keeps you alive in crisis can kill you once you are free.
One must not choose to die, though one must die anyway.

—TANYA TAGAQ, *Split Tooth*

I Love Them So!

⇒⊁⊱⊰⊰

AFTER MY MOTHER'S memorial service, my aunt and my grandmothers all called to wish me a happy Mother's Day.

"I'm not a mother," I said. I thought they had made a mistake—confused me with my sister and her son.

"No," they said, "your sisters. You're their mother now."*

I HAVE NEVER wanted children; I am terrified of the thought of motherhood.

Sometimes, I fantasized about a little girl, three or four years old, who I held in a kitchen with yellow curtains. I hooked one arm around her waist and rested her on my hip as I stirred a pot on the stove, but that was as far as the fantasy went.

My grandmother always believed I would change my mind. As a high school graduation present, she crocheted me a blue baby blanket, though I was neither pregnant nor planning to be. Years later, I would fold it into a kind of cat bed. Still, anytime I called, she asked when I planned to get married, when I would have children, and I answered never. I never wanted, or would want, to be a mother.

SOME DAYS, I think I should not have meddled with my mother's things. No bundle of sage could protect me. I am ghost-sick, pos-

---

* September 25, 1995. "I know deep in my heart one day the girls will be back in my life."

sessed by every wrong thing she was unable to bring into balance in her life.

SOME DAYS, I believe I should have buried her suitcase in Dale's garden—lost these histories forever in Florida's black earth.

Most days, I do not believe I know how to care for my mother's ghost.

[Little Sheep]

⁓⤬⁓

MY COUSIN-SISTER CALLED me a few weeks after I moved to Tucson. Sobbing, at four-thirty in the morning. She found out her boyfriend was cheating. She started the fight. "I will come get you," I told her. "I will bring you home with me."

THE NAVAJO FAIR was in town. People claimed spots all along the parade route in Window Rock and planted their tents and chairs along the side of the main road. We skipped the powwow and the ceremonials held that night; instead, we stayed home, bundled under blankets in her room, and competed for the highest *Spider Solitaire* score. We fell asleep watching *A Bug's Life,* our heads facing in opposite directions.

The next morning, I woke before my cousin-sister and slipped out the door with a pair of military binoculars my cousin-brother brought back from his service in Iraq. My aunt's dog, Toro, followed me down the twisting dirt road and into the flowering sagebrush hills. He followed his nose off the path, under bushes, over piles of gravel and rock. He missed a pair of cottontails, who bolted out from under my feet as I crossed the same ground minutes later. They reached the safety of a hidden burrow before he even turned around.

The trees that morning were full of birds: thrashers and songbirds and, overhead, a single croaking raven. I called Toro's name, and he circled back to heel, bumping his nose into my empty hand. I patted his rib cage, scratched under his collar, talked cheerfully to him and the birds and the morning as we walked back to my aunt's house.

When my cousin-sister woke, we packed her bags into my truck and left for Tucson. As we drove down I-40, my cousin-sister pointed out our family's allotment, a small piece of land intended for too many of Pauline Tom's heirs. She pointed out the cemetery where our grandmother was buried. The cemetery was barely distinguishable to me from the rest of the landscape, and when I followed her gaze, I saw only the stark white faces of the headstones and the silver glint of a ribbon in the wind.

"When you leave a graveyard, you have to do a blessing," she said. "Or the spirit could follow you home."

I thought of the smudge sticks, the bundles of dried sage, that I had found in my mother's things. I burned them for days after returning from the hospital. I burned them after I went through her letters and her photographs. I burned sage, even though I didn't consider myself superstitious, even though I knew no bundle of sage could protect me from the things I might discover.

My cousin-sister stared out the window for a few quiet moments, then looked at me. "What's the difference between a spirit and a ghost?"

"I don't know," I said honestly.

"Neither do I," she said, "but I don't believe in ghosts."

MY COUSIN-SISTER STAYED with me a week. I caught the flu from my freshman students, and I told her to keep her distance, but she said she wouldn't get sick. We spent our days curled up on the couch streaming *Shameless*. She rested her head on my shoulder, on my hip.

A court date was scheduled, back on the reservation. She told me she needed to attend it, or a warrant would be issued for her arrest. I agreed to drive her home on the twenty-first, after my morning classes ended, and I realized I would be with my family, on the reservation, on the second anniversary of my mother's death—not by plan but by circumstance.

The heavy rains of Tropical Depression Sixteen-E followed us for most of the drive, but as soon as we crossed onto the reservation, the rain stopped. By the time we arrived, my aunt had already fallen asleep, but she leapt out of bed as soon as she heard us walk through the door. She scurried into the kitchen and served us heaping plates of creamed chicken over rice, with green beans and corn on the side.

My cousin sister's thumbs moved rapidly across the keys on her phone. She carried her empty plate to the sink, then disappeared into her room.

I followed my aunt to the couch; over the sound of the TV, I could hear my cousin-sister quietly giggling on the phone.

I wanted to believe she wasn't talking to her boyfriend, but when I walked into her room to get ready for sleep, she mumbled something into the receiver and quickly ended the call.

"Who was that?" I asked.

She smiled at me, a smile somewhere between innocent and mischievous. "Who do you think?"

"Your boyfriend," I said.

"Yeah," she said guiltily, but trying not to laugh. She spun an elaborate story—that she was talking to one of her friends, who hadn't heard what had happened, but that my cousin-sister's boyfriend had asked the friend to ask her for his mother's set of keys— that reminded me of a story Eileen might devise. My cousin-sister told me she was embarrassed about the fight, and she didn't want to tell anyone what happened, and so she called her boyfriend to settle things instead.

I picked up a pillow and turned to walk back into the living room, to sleep on the couch.

"No, wait!" she said. "You sleep in here. You're sick."

"I don't mind," I said.

"You sleep here," she insisted.

She tucked me in, under a pile of blankets. I watched her grab a pair of socks out of the dresser before she closed the door behind her. I pretended not to know where she was going, or what she planned to do.

But I couldn't sleep. I rotated slowly in bed so that my head pointed north, then east, then south, then west. It was something I did on sleepless nights, a way of tricking my body into falling asleep, but it didn't work. My cough kept me awake.

I untangled my legs from the blankets, climbed out of bed, and walked into the dark living room. "Are you awake?" I asked, touching the pile of blankets on the couch, but the peak caved under my hand. I was surprised I hadn't heard my cousin-sister leave.

I returned to bed and fell asleep.

I DREAMT OF a two-story sandstone motel, its three square walls opening onto the desert. A sun set between two mountains, and heavy drapes were drawn across all the windows. My mother and my aunt and all my sisters were running in and out of the rooms, slamming doors, shouting at one another from the landings. I understood that each door was a choice, each room a potential future, and that my mother's and my aunt's and my sisters' doors were closed to me. Standing on the landing and looking into the sun, I noticed the figure of a solitary woman in the desert. She wore a loose blouse and a long skirt, cinched by an elaborate concho belt, and though I'd never met her, I knew she was Pauline Tom, our gnomon, casting a long, indecipherable shadow on our lives.

I woke to the sound of water lapping stone. I sat up in my cousin-sister's bed and peeked through the blinds to watch the rain carve pools in the red clay. If I were better rested, I would have walked into the hills and looked for waterlogged birds, but I was tired, too tired.

I wandered into the living room, where my aunt sat on the couch on top of my cousin-sister's blankets. "She left last night," my aunt said, pushing a pad of paper toward me.

I picked it up and read: "Went to Gallup. Need to get pads and face wash. Should be back soon."

My cousin-sister wrote a number on the bottom of the note, but when my aunt tried to call it, no one answered.

"She prolly went to see *that guy*," my aunt sighed.

My aunt asked me to follow her into the kitchen; she told me to sit and began boiling water on the stove. "I heard you coughing *all night*," she said, dropping bundles of Navajo tea into the pot. She stirred and strained the drink, then set a full mug in front of me. "This will make you feel better."

"Thank you," I said, hugging my hands around the warm mug. I blew tight ripples over the surface of the golden-brown tea.

She set a plate of French toast in front of me, then told me she needed to run an errand for a friend, but asked me to come by the hair salon later—she wanted to give me a present before I left for Tucson.

I told her I would stop by.

I crawled back into bed after I finished my breakfast. I tried to read for class, but I couldn't concentrate on the book. One of my professors, Ander Monson, had assigned us to keep track of the day, September 22—to record everything that happened in an essay— and so I jotted down a few notes. Then I walked to the front porch and stared at the muddy front yard, where my aunt and her neighbor had spent the previous day clearing out the summer weeds. Toro made a rabbit's nest of them.

I crooned his name from the porch, and he lifted his head and fixed me with red and watery eyes, but did not move.

I walked a few steps into the yard and called his name again. He stood slowly on quivering legs.

Concerned, I walked over to him, and he leaned the entire weight of his body against my legs. "Toro," I whispered, and I traced the black line between his eyes, smoothed my hands over his head and down his sides. I remembered the stories my cousin-sister had told me. All the times Toro had been hit, flipped over the hoods of cars. Gotten up, shaken it off. I wondered if he had been hit again. "It's so hard, I know," I said, rubbing his soft ears. "It's so hard." My aunt wouldn't take him to the vet. He was a rez dog now.

Toro took a few steps away from me and lay down in his nest of weeds. He curled into a tight ball, with his back to me. There was nothing I could give him—nothing I felt I could do.

I walked back into the house and waited for my cousin by the screen door.

She told me she hadn't seen her boyfriend when she finally returned home. She said she went to Shorty's, across the street, and helped him set mouse traps in the middle of the night. He couldn't do it himself, she told me. He kept catching his fingers. She would tell me if she saw her boyfriend.

I wanted to believe her.

ON THE DRIVE out of town, I stopped at my aunt's work, a salon and flower shop that operated out of a trailer. She offered to cut my hair, which was too long and breaking at the ends. She washed it, massaging the shampoo into my scalp, then led me back to her chair and draped a pink cloth around my shoulders. I watched her reflection in the mirror, dividing and redividing my hair and constantly adjusting the black banana clip that held it on top of my head.

"This is where I was when I found out your mom died," she said, suddenly. "I went in the back and cried and cried."

I wasn't sure what to say, so I said nothing.

"I'm glad you could be here today," she said, as if I had planned my visit intentionally.

She fought the tears in her eyes as she finished cutting my hair.

Before I left, my aunt gave me a glass vase full of plastic purple and yellow flowers—a memorial gift, to bring home with me. Tucked inside the arrangement was a card with a message written in my aunt's handwriting, so similar to my mother's perfect script: "Missing you. We Love You." Missing, always.

ON THE DRIVE home, I looked for the cemetery my cousin-sister pointed out to me the previous week. I scanned the side of the highway—watching for the headstones, the silver ribbon. I imagined stopping and visiting my grandmother's grave, even though I didn't know the blessing. I wasn't worried about spirits or ghosts. But I didn't recognize the cemetery or my family's land.

[Beauty]

IN TUCSON, I tried to fill my life with beauty. I bought a sunshine-yellow beach cruiser, and as I pedaled to school in the mornings, I paid attention to the hummingbirds buzzing around cactus blossoms, the verdins hopping in the mesquite, the Gila woodpeckers scaling saguaro and palm.

On the weekends, I drove into the desert, sometimes alone and sometimes with the new friends I made through the MFA program. We hiked up mountains and through canyon and wash. I filled my life with poetry and literature and attended readings at the university and around town.

I shared pieces of my book project in my nonfiction workshops, until I received a feedback letter from one of my cohort, who told me that I sounded angry; that I should learn how to forgive my father. He suggested I seek therapy. I cried for hours.

When my mother had visited me in Pennsylvania for my college graduation, she'd attended a reading hosted by the school's undergraduate literary journal, which had published one of my essays about my father and his racism; the discoveries I had been making about my Diné heritage; and my mother's inability, or unwillingness, to aid me on my quest. After the reading, she was uncharacteristically quiet.

I asked her what was wrong.

"Why would you write something like that?" she said: an accusation, not a question. She would not meet my eyes. I had never felt my mother's anger directed at me before, and I lost all words. I did not write another essay, did not write at all, until after she died.

A few weeks after the workshop, I started seeing a psychiatrist through the school's counseling center. They assigned me to an ancient white man, a wizened turtle, who could hardly stay awake. I told him I was anxious about my book and my degree. I told him I was struggling with my mother's death. I told him about my father and my sisters and about my worries for them. As I talked, his eyelids fluttered, and his balding head nodded up and down. When I stopped talking, he startled awake and shuffled the papers on his desk. "You seem like you're handling things remarkably well," he said. I did not feel as if I was handling things remarkably well, but I thanked him. I kept talking even after his eyes closed again, though I knew it wouldn't help.

[Nursing Home]

THE SUMMER AFTER my first year in Tucson, I joined two of my cohort for a field study in writing on Grand Manan, a Canadian island floating off the coast of New Brunswick, across the international boundary line from Maine. For two weeks, we were given the freedom to explore the island and write about the local community, a traditional fishing village facing radical changes as herring populations crashed in the Bay of Fundy. In our first few days on the island, we drove past fishing wharfs, traditional herring weirs, and shuttered smokehouses. We visited dark warehouses that housed lobster, hibernating in the icy cold. The lobster industry exploded as the herring populations collapsed, and we met high school–aged boys who made small fortunes on lobster boats.

My colleagues opted to take a whale-watching trip, but I signed up for a bird-watching tour instead. Our destination was a seabird breeding colony on Machias Seal Island, which was little more than a jut of rock in the middle of the sea. Only the first fifteen on board were allowed to disembark, to sit in narrow blinds and watch the seabirds up close, but the captain offered to take those remaining— me and two others—in a skiff around the island. The water was calm and flat. The captain let the skiff idle and started making a strange, rattling sound in his throat. A handful of puffins became curious, paddling closer in nervous circles with their carrot-orange feet.

On the return trip, I noticed I had missed a call from my father— more than one—though I figured he was probably drunk. I waited until I got back to the bed-and-breakfast to call him.

He told me my grandmother hadn't slept in days—that she was hallucinating. She was surrounded by her young children, by people who weren't there. "She lives in New Jersey now," he said, laughing.

I tried to laugh with him, but I was worried. "Does anyone know what's wrong?"

"The doctors don't know anything," he complained, though he suspected it was a reaction to her new medication.

He told me to enjoy my trip, though I found it almost impossible to relax.

The next day we visited Kent Island where there was a nesting colony of Leach's storm petrels. The island's researchers nicknamed their nesting grounds "the Shire" after the fairy-green moss that blanketed their underground burrows. We followed a student intern to the site and watched her pull a sleeping petrel out of its burrow and pop it headfirst into a cardboard toilet paper tube. She weighed it and took a sample of its blood, and she recited a few facts about their feeding and mating habits, though I had forgotten to bring anything beyond my phone with which to take notes.

My father called me again that night to tell me my grandmother had been admitted to a nursing home for observation, but they only had a bed for a man, not a woman, and she had been sent home again. He said he hadn't slept in days, either, but his voice was filled with a kind of manic energy. He railed against the ineptitude of the doctors, the nursing home, and his sister, who was trying to wrest the control of my grandmother's caretaking from him. "She doesn't care about your grandma," he insisted; he believed she was only in it for whatever little money my grandmother might have in the end.

The next morning, I hiked to a waterfall and spotted a thrush, almost perfectly camouflaged in the dense undergrowth. I leveled my binoculars on his round black eye, and for as long as I watched him, he didn't move or make a sound.

My father called twice, but I didn't answer. He left a message telling me he thought he'd figured out the road map to artificial intelligence and that my grandmother should be a whole lot better by Monday. And then he revised his statement to tell me she wasn't faring much better at all.

I decided to derail my return trip to Tucson. I rented a car in Maine and drove to Pennsylvania through a major thunderstorm. I should have stopped—there were times the rain fell faster than the wipers could clear the windshield; fell so hard I could barely see the brake lights of the car in front of me. I passed a fresh accident every few miles: fenders smashed and hoods crumpled and an RV tumbled cleanly onto its side. In the mountains, I detoured off the highway for miles—a semi had crashed, and gallons of sulfuric acid washed across the road. I should have stopped, but each time I felt my tires leave the ground, planing over the torrential rain, I simply lifted my foot off the gas pedal and held my course.

"Did the storm pass?" my grandmother asked when I walked into her hospital room. She looked not at me but through me, as if I weren't really there. "I feel like I was waitin' on it."

I told her it had.

My aunt pulled me into the hallway to update me on my grandmother's condition: what the doctors had and hadn't said, and what they wanted to do. They believed the hallucinations were the side effect of a medication, but that she also exhibited early signs of dementia. My grandmother's oldest sister, Jessie, had Alzheimer's; I remembered visiting her in the nursing home when we were kids. I told my aunt I understood.

She asked me to stay the night with my grandmother in the nursing home, because she was worried Grandma wasn't getting enough sleep, or that the nurses weren't responding to her calls.

I agreed to stay.

After my aunt left, I sat in the chair beside my grandmother's bed and watched the Westerns playing quietly on the far side of the room. My grandmother dozed until ten that night, then woke suddenly—her eyes wide and nervous. I offered her my hand, and she took it, stroking the back with her thumb. It was an intimacy that was foreign to our relationship, and it made me slightly uncomfortable.

"It hurts," my grandmother breathed through her teeth, all sharp ss-ss-ss's. "Help me."

I told her I would be back. I paced the halls trying to find a nurse, but the nurse I found told me she couldn't give my grandmother anything for the pain—she had already received her full dose earlier that day. I returned to my grandmother's room and tried to explain, but she didn't understand what I was saying.

"Help me," she repeated.

I helped her turn, from her right side to her left to her right side again, but nothing seemed to help. Neither of us slept.

The dawn flushed the windows pink, and I told my grandmother I would be back. I drove to her apartment to pick up my father, who agreed to stay with her that morning. I dropped him off and then returned to my grandmother's apartment to sleep. I slept fitfully, my knees rattling the metal railing attached to the side of her bed each time I turned under the sheets.

My aunt convinced the nurses to change my grandmother's dosing schedule, but she asked me to stay the night again.

Again, my grandmother slept until ten, and then she woke, complaining about the pain. "It hurts. I'm uncomfortable," she repeated, the hard consonants of her words digging under my skin.

If my mother had the patience to be a caretaker, I knew I did not. I tried to help her get comfortable. I shifted her weight back and forth with the sheet, like I'd watched the nurses do. But again, no position was right, and five minutes after I rested my grandmother on one side, she asked me to help her roll over again. The frustration turned to anger, and I dropped my head and groaned, "You aren't going to be comfortable."

My grandmother slowly turned her head toward me and stared into my eyes. "When did you get so mean?"

I shook my head and walked out of her room, down the hall,

past the residents who were parked outside their rooms in their wheelchairs. I watched a woman creep past the nurses' station, her shuffling feet pulling her wheelchair inch by inch. The nurse seated by the computer seemed to ignore the woman and stared at her screen.

The next morning, I picked up my father again, but I didn't even bother trying to return to my grandmother's to sleep. My father wheeled my grandmother out of her room and outside, to sit beneath the shade of the porte-cochère. In the empty lot across the street, a bulldozer ripped the land open to sky. A flock of barn swallows dipped and dove above its hand. My grandmother fell asleep with her chin on her chest, her shoulders bowed in.

I celebrated my thirtieth birthday in the nursing home with my grandmother. We sat together in her room and watched old reruns on TV. At lunch, I watched her try to pick up a toothpick off her tray, and just as I reached over to help, she pinned it between her two fingers and slid it into her mouth.

"You got it," I said, surprised.

She leaned back to inspect the piece of food she excavated from between her teeth. "You never know when the next miracle's going to happen," she laughed.

I left the nursing home early that evening; my aunt told me she didn't think I needed to pull another all-nighter. I drove an hour north of the city and bought myself an ice cream cone. I had invited my father to join me, but he declined. He tried to call me later—drunk.

He was already at the nursing home when I arrived the next morning. He had spent the night sleeping in the bushes outside. He asked me for a ride home so he could babysit my nephew, who flew past both of us and straight to the television when he arrived.

My father sent me to the grocery store for peanut butter and jelly, one of the few things my nephew would eat. I spent ten minutes wandering, lost, unable to find the right aisle.

That night, my nephew sat beside me on the couch. I sat very still and avoided his eyes, as if he were a cat. He took one of my hands and touched his side. "Tickle," he told me, and I wiggled my fingers below his ribs and behind his knees while he played a game on his Kindle. If I stopped, he would grab my hand again.

That night, as I tried to fall asleep, I listened to my nephew's voice in the dark: "Don't go. Wait. Espere. No se vaya. Don't go." English and Spanish, backward and forward. He sang, soft and quiet: "I love you. You love me. We're a happy family." I wondered what he understood of family, and if he missed his mother, too.

[I Tried to Say]

—⊹—

THEY SENT MY father to me again three months later. My aunt bought him a train ticket and sent him on his way. Eileen met him during his stop in Pittsburgh to bring him food, bottles of water, clean clothes, and a pair of work boots. All he had to do was get on the train. Instead, he sent me a text message to say he wasn't coming. "I love you too much," he said.

Drunk, he called Eileen, who left work to go find him. She held me on the phone as she ran around the train station; crying, she kept repeating, "All he had to do was get on the train!" She finally found him, drunk and harassing a group of other homeless men.

She started yelling at him, and he yelled back, "I just want to stay here with my new friends!"

I imagined her waving the cellphone in the air with one hand while she pulled on him with the other.

"We don't know him," an unfamiliar voice said, and I covered my mouth to try and muffle a laugh.

I listened to the static thudding of something bumping against the phone's microphone. Then the call dropped.

Eileen called me back later to tell me she bought him a new train ticket. She bought him food and tried to help him find his luggage, which had gone missing, without luck. She sat with him in the station until his next train arrived.

AN OLDER MAN I met on Craigslist lived with me. He was an engineer who'd lost his job, then moved back West to be near his son.

He reminded me a little of "Weird Al" Yankovic, with his curly mop of brown hair, and he offered to pay three months up front, which I should have recognized as a warning sign. But he mostly kept to himself—closing himself in his room, brewing beer in the kitchen on the weekends. It took weeks for our relationship to unravel.

He couldn't find or hold a good job, and he spent more and more time around the apartment. One afternoon, after he'd had too much to drink, he cornered me in the kitchen and started ranting about his ex-wife and his mother-in-law, who pressed charges against him for physical assault. He didn't deny hurting her—it was clear from the story he had.

I marveled that I had found a man so like my dad.

Not long after the three months he paid in advance, he stopped paying me rent. He promised that he was working on it. He offered to buy me groceries with his food stamps. He paid me portions of the rent he owed, but not all. It made me feel less guilty about my father crashing on our couch.

Before my father arrived, I explained the situation to him. I told him he could continue brewing beer in the apartment, but I asked that he not give any to my dad.

MY FATHER DIDN'T even pretend to stop drinking. He spent most of his days drinking downtown, and then would come back to my apartment to pass out on the couch. He met a woman at the public library, who he brought back to my apartment most nights. They slept in a pile of blankets on my floor, and they claimed to be in love. They told me they were going to get married.

"I love you as much as I love your dad," she told me.

I refused to look at her, or even meet her eyes. The love of an addict is a trap.

She told me she was my mother now. When I said I didn't want a mother, she cried to my father, "She hates me!" She was always crying.

My father called me a bitch.

"*Send him to me,*" my mother had said. "*I'll take care of him.*" But my father was too old, too grown, for any of that to make sense.

My schoolwork suffered. I stopped writing. In class, I talked too often and too loudly about my father, because I did not know who or how to ask for help.

One afternoon, I came home and found my father, his girlfriend, and my roommate all drinking together in my kitchen. As soon as I walked in the door, they scattered.

I told my father he needed to leave. He tried to joke his way out of trouble, but I demanded he give me my spare key, and then I kicked him out.

My roommate ventured into the kitchen an hour later to refill his glass, and I confronted him about giving my father alcohol, about his missing rent. He told me he had nowhere to go; that he couldn't stay with his son.

"I don't care," I said. "I want you out."

"I could make this hell for you," he said, his voice rising. He swung his glass above his head and bounced on his toes. "I could make you evict me and drag this out for a fucking month."

I didn't move. I kept my voice even and looked into his eyes. "Are you threatening me?"

"I'm not threatening you," he said, backing down. "I'm just telling you the way it is."

"No," I said, standing. "You threatened me, and you need to leave. That's what's happening now."

The next morning, sober, my roommate tried to apologize—to wheedle his way back into my good graces—but it wouldn't work. I gave him a few days to find another place to stay. I knew I would never see the money he owed, but I was willing to shoulder the cost to live, finally, alone.

MY FATHER AND his girlfriend didn't move far from my apartment—they slept in the park across the street, until the resident meth addict chased them out. They moved to the sidewalk in front of the library instead, a few blocks from my house.

Every few days, my father brought me items in penance— packages of dried beans, ramen, and traveler-sized toiletries donated to the shelter. My spare key disappeared, but I didn't bother to ask for it back.

He stayed away until winter, when the nightly temperatures dropped below freezing. He called and begged to stay at my apartment, just for one night.

I told him he could but asked him to please, please, please be sober.

He brought his girlfriend with him. I retreated to my bedroom and cracked the door—just wide enough for my cat to come and go. I played a videogame with the headphones askew on my head so I could keep an ear on the door, their muffled voices. The toilet flushed. My father mumbled something, and his girlfriend whined his name.

I set my headphones on the desk and crept closer to my door.

"I'm horny," I heard my father say.

"I love you," she said. When he didn't answer, she said it again.

"I want to stick my dick in your pussy," he said.

I closed my eyes. She repeated his name. The shower started to run, and the sound of the water interfered with their voices, but I thought I heard her say, "Please don't hit me again."

I turned on my stereo, then turned it off. I paced to my window and then back to my door. The water turned off, and the bathroom door opened, and the door to the spare bedroom closed. The futon creaked under their weight.

He told her he wanted to cum inside her.

I wanted to stop listening, but I waited for her answer: She was trying to tell him no.

I grabbed my keys and ran out of the apartment. I sat in my car behind my building and called the local police, but I didn't know how to tell the officer what I heard.

"My dad is drunk," I said, aware of how small I sounded.

"Is he violent?" he asked.

"I just want him out of my apartment," I said. "He won't leave."

"Does he live there?"

"No. Not really. He's homeless. He's just staying with me."

"Unfortunately," he sighed, "if you want to evict him, you're going to have to go through your landlord."

After my long silence he said, "We can send an officer to the house."

I didn't really want the police to show up at my apartment. I didn't want my father to know I was snitching on him, or for him to accuse me of betraying him again. He would deny everything, and so would she.

"That's okay," I said, and I hung up the phone before I started to cry. The leaves of the gum trees whispered above my head.

[Little Tweets]

THE WOMAN WHO raised my sister Alex messaged me and Eileen a few days before Christmas. "I told her about you guys," she said, adding, "but it's her decision if she wants to talk to you."

When I opened Instagram, I noticed a new follow notification. Alex didn't send me a message, but she liked a blurry photograph of a bird I posted, a Hutton's vireo, its olive-yellow belly set in contrast with the bare white branches of a tree. She liked a photograph I took of a Gila woodpecker, its black-and-white-barred back peeking between the leaves of a mesquite.

Eileen asked if Alex had contacted me.

"Not yet," I said.

Eileen copied a message Alex sent to her, warning Eileen she couldn't just barge into her life. She told her she didn't want a relationship with her, but especially with me, because we had gone behind her mother's back. "She's the world to me," Alex had said. "She's all I know, and it's going to stay that way."

"Did you message her first?" I asked.

"I liked a couple of her pictures and commented on one," she said. "I couldn't help myself."

I had noticed. Eileen had posted a memorial to her dead betta fish, Dexter.

"She was like, 'Good! I'm glad your fish is dead!'" Eileen laughed. "'I hope everything in your life dies!'"

I laughed, hysterically. "She's prolly all fucked up over this," I said, quieting. I realized I had likely pushed too hard—that I hadn't considered what our sister might have needed.

"I think she just needs time," Eileen agreed.

I had been used to the enthusiasm of our youngest sister, who I met—once—after finding her adoptive mother's phone number in a card they sent to my mother before she died. Her family was planning to visit Florida, and they asked if my mother would want to spend some time with them while they were there. I wasn't sure they would want to hear from me—I spent days agonizing about whether I should call. But her mother sounded enthusiastic when she answered, and my sister sent me frequent text messages from her mother's phone. She asked me to send her pictures of myself and my room in Tucson; she asked me to send her pictures of my cats. She sent me pictures of her bedroom and her dog, and she invited me to play games with her online, like *Club Penguin*. I followed her through the virtual town, and she proudly showed me her decorated igloo and introduced me to her pet, a cherry-red Koosh ball with eyes.

For Christmas, I mailed her one of our mother's turquoise necklaces, and I mailed Eileen a woven red-and-green belt. I wondered what I would have to offer any of them when there was nothing left of my mother to divide.

[Solitary]

FENTON JOHNSON, ONE of my professors, developed a theory about me through my writing: that I was a solitary, like other figures and writers he admired. I was flattered. In his essay "Going It Alone," Fenton writes, "Spinsterhood is a calling, a destiny."

When I imagined my future unspooling before me, I pictured myself alone in the desert. I walk down a dusty trail; the sun warms my shoulders. I hear a rustle and turn my binoculars to leaf, to lizard, to bird. I watch the yawn of a pink mouth or the slow stretch of a wing within the peace of a millisecond, extended beyond the space of a millisecond. "The great, incomparable reward of being alone is the opportunity," Fenton writes, "to encounter the great silence at the core of being, a silence that is both uniquely mine and one with the background hum of the universe."

A FEW MONTHS after my sister Alex added me on social media, we took our first baby steps into a relationship with each other. Then I offered her a gigantic leap: a plane ticket to visit me in Tucson for a month. She accepted. She booked a one-way ticket to Tucson, arriving in April, and we planned a road trip through the states—through the mountains of Colorado, through Pittsburgh to see Eileen—for her return trip to Florida.

I offered her the futon in the spare bedroom, still cluttered with the junk my father had carried home.

I introduced her to some of my friends. We walked Fourth Avenue and investigated one of the local coffee shops. We visited the

International Wildlife Museum, a taxidermy museum, where the stuffed animals were arranged in lifelike dioramas: wolves hunting; brown bears fishing for orange salmon in a fake pool; a bobcat reaching for a quail against a snowy backdrop. An entire room was dedicated to the mounted heads of dozens of species of antelope. Alex posed in front of each exhibit and asked me to take her picture for Instagram, but my enthusiasm quickly waned, and she could feel it.

I was too busy with school. Too preoccupied with my father, who still existed on the periphery of my life. I was inaccessible, as if living in a state of hibernation, storing my energy for the next catastrophe.

I did not know how to be a sister to her.

We spent more time alone in our rooms. She talked on the phone with her boyfriend for hours. She missed him and couldn't wait to be home. They argued—sometimes playfully, sometimes angrily—about the strength and virtue of their longing.

BEFORE ALEX AND I left for Florida, I went looking for my father downtown. I found his girlfriend sitting on a bench across from the library. She told me he would be back soon—he had left to sell some cans at the junkyard.

"We've been sober two weeks," she told me while we waited.

"That's good," I said, trying to sound encouraging. It was the first time I had seen her without tears in her eyes.

She looked down at her feet, and then at me. "You were right to kick us out."

I didn't know if I should thank her. I nodded and then walked slowly toward the corner of the street to wait for my father. A few minutes later, he arrived, wearing the key to my apartment on a lanyard around his neck.

"I wondered where that was," I said, even knowing where it had been all along.

"I didn't use it," he said, shrugging. "I kept it safe."

I told him I would be leaving for two weeks. One of my friends would be staying in my apartment and feeding my cats.

ALEX AND I left for our road trip in the middle of the night so we could watch the sun rise over the Grand Canyon's sandstone cliffs. We arrived in lavender, and I nosed carefully around the elk that foraged along the park's roads. Recovering from a migraine, I napped in the car while Alex wandered the rim.

From the Grand Canyon, we drove east toward our grand-mother's house on the reservation. We lost phone reception. She stared out the window at the rocks and the dirt and complained about being bored.

We stopped at a canyon, advertised by a brown tourism sign, as we crossed onto the reservation. I took a short video of her sitting beneath the Navajo Nation's flag. "It's really hot," she says, squint-ing into the sun and complaining, deadpan, through a smile. "My bangs are sweaty. I'm going to die at any moment."

I stopped filming and bent over laughing.

We walked down a short path to another canyon. I handed her my binoculars and pointed at the swallows and the crows riding the wind.

We arrived at our aunt's by midafternoon, but she was at work, and all the lights in the house were dark. I parked along the road and walked around back and knocked on my cousin-sister's win-dow. She yelled my name in delight and ran to the back door to let us in. We wrapped each other in a tight hug, though her seven-months-swollen belly held us apart.

For lunch we took her to McDonald's, where she complained about her mother and her mother's drinking; about her boyfriend and their constant arguments.

We returned to my grandmother's house. I told them I needed to sleep. I would be driving again all the next day because Alex didn't have a license. I lay down on the air mattress in the living room and fell asleep listening to my aunt and my sisters talk.

Early the next morning, we drove north. We stopped at a flea market in Farmington, where Alex tried her first frybread. We continued toward Denver, through mountains still packed with snow. I charged a fancy hotel in downtown Denver to my credit card, and we gorged on pasta and bread at an Italian restaurant. I returned to the hotel room early, but Alex went looking for Voodoo Doughnut and brought back one of their signatures for me.

We drove long, slow hours across Nebraska, through the endless cornfields of Iowa and Illinois. We stopped in Chicago to stay with my childhood friend Lexi, who worked at the Adler Planetarium and gave us tickets to see her show. Alex and I walked the public gardens along the waterfront. I took a photograph of a seagull, perched atop the infamous silver bean.

We arrived in Pittsburgh the next day. Eileen took Alex to the train yard where she'd squatted when she was homeless. I stayed behind and graded papers with her new betta fish.

We only stayed in Pittsburgh for a day, and then we were off to Florida in a single sixteen-hour shot. We crossed the Florida border in the middle of the night. I parked at a rest stop to catch a few hours' sleep, though Alex begged me to keep going. She was anxious to be home, to sleep in her own bed, but I couldn't keep my eyes open. We pulled into her driveway a little after ten.

ALEX'S MOTHER MADE me uncomfortable. She seemed to talk around me and refused to meet my eyes. They offered to let me sleep on their couch, but I rented a hotel room instead.

The next day, Alex and I drove to Lake Worth, to Bryant Park, where my mother had been living before she died. There was no one around. We wandered through the clean white pavilion, where my mother might have slept, but I found no evidence that anyone lived there at all. Alex and I sat together on the concrete seawall and watched a flock of ibis, pure white birds with pink faces and curved beaks, graze in the park's green grass. I wondered if I should have come at night instead.

The next day, we hardly saw each other. I drove around my old neighborhoods, searching for evidence of past lives.

AMONG MY MOTHER's photographs I found an envelope of negatives, slipped inside Eckerd's plastic sleeves. They were numbered one through twenty-five, the number of exposures on a disposable camera. Frustrated by all the unrecognizable faces and places I encountered in her developed photos—frustrated by the difficulty of translating negative space into life and color—I almost threw them out. But as I held the strip of negatives up to the light, one frame in particular caught my attention. I recognized my mother's and Fran's silhouettes, side by side. I could make out, in caramel and cream, the distinct, pale hollow of their exposed breasts.

I became obsessed with holding that photograph in my hands. I spent two hundred dollars on a special backlit scanner to digitize the negatives myself. The resulting images were grainy—the plastic film had already begun to degrade, the colors shifting and beginning to fade. I discovered the photograph belonged to a series of photographs, taken by my mother in 1995 at the house off Military Trail where my mother had lived with my father, my uncle, and Fran.

That period of time was confusing to me as a child. My parents were separated but living together. My father was dating Fran, and my mother was dating my father's brother, but when my grandmother took us to visit, everyone seemed happy there. My mother had given me copies of some of the photographs at one point; I recognized one someone had taken of the four of them posing together next to a concrete structure, which I came to realize was a grill. In another, my sister and I, smiling, stand in front of my father and the banyan tree. He squeezes us in his arms.

At that house, my sister and I helped my father paint one of his vans. He gave us buckets of old paint and jars of glitter, which we threw in fistfuls across our metal canvas. We climbed on top of the van and slid around the roof on our asses. When our father sobered up, he repainted the van gray, but kept a panel of color and glitter around the middle.

In my mother's things I found physical copies of some of these photographs, but not all. She did not keep the pictures of her and my uncle—their relationship was short lived. She did not keep the pictures of my father or of Fran. But she did hold on to the negatives. Why I can never know, but it feels to me as if there were something she couldn't let go of.

Within her photographs, I recognize myself in my mother in strange places, in the perspective she chose—a pointed shadow, a rut of tires, the contrast of scrubby grass and pale gray sand. Not accidental exposures but a fraction of a moment that caught her eye.

The final photograph in the series is candid; I can tell by the awkward angle. A rainbow-striped lawn chair dominates the foreground. My father, wearing a red flannel and holding a can of beer, stares at the ground and away from the photographer, my mother. The door leading inside the house, a shadow.

I DROVE AROUND the neighborhoods on both sides of Military Trail, but I could not find the house where they lived. I found the lot of the apartment my uncle shared with his new girlfriend, Kerry, though the airport had bought and demolished the entire block. I drove in circles until I found a dirt road, chalky and white like Nokomis. I got out of the car and pressed the white dust between my hands.

I texted Alex, asking if she wanted to visit one of the Everglades parks with me, but she declined.

On the drive down, I unexpectedly passed and recognized Faith Farm, one of my father's many rehabs.

I arrived at the park in the late afternoon. I followed a boardwalk into cypress and fern. There were no birds, no bird songs. The waterlogged earth swallowed all sound except for a strange knocking, somewhere far away. A flash of red caught my eye, and I stopped to watch a lizard flare its dewlap, shining bright with its own blood, in a small patch of sun. I began to feel certain I would die.

I hurried back to my car and drove down the road to the end of the park, where a wharf met the true swamp of the Everglades. A posted sign on a shuttered shack advertised kayak and fan boat rides. I walked down to the water, where families with coolers and fishing poles gathered, and leaned against the railing. I spotted the ridged head of a small gator floating toward the reeds like a piece of driftwood.

I eavesdropped on the conversations around me. A man told a boy about the fifteen-foot alligator that lived beneath the wharf and sometimes stole fish. They called him George. I leaned over the railing and looked into the water, murky and dark, and could just make out the outline of his massive body: the swell of his stomach and the point of his snout. His eyes closed tight.

I walked away from the families, to the other side of the parking lot, and sat cross-legged on a floating dock to watch the sun set over the cattails.

THE MORNING I left, Alex and I met at one of her favorite coffee shops. I sat down with her and her boyfriend for a few minutes while I ate a croissant. When I stood up to leave, she refused a hug and said, "I don't want to watch you go."

I was surprised to hear the quaver of tears in her voice.

I told her it was okay, that we would see each other soon. I cleared my plate and mug off the table and walked out the door. I did not glance over my shoulder to see if she had changed her mind, if she had looked for me.

still cruising

⌁⌁⌁✦⌁⌁⌁

ON MY RETURN to Arizona, I drove through the pine forests of
the Florida panhandle into Alabama, across water and marsh. I followed a route similar to the one my mother had taken when she
and Alex's father drove to Arizona for her brother Dundee's funeral.* I stayed the night with a friend in Missouri, then picked up a
hitchhiker at a gas station on the Mississippi-Louisiana border: a
greasy kitten that I watched try to climb into the engine of a parked
car. A woman with a van full of kids helped me catch him, though
she told me she couldn't take him home because of her dogs. On
the road, he climbed onto my shoulder and cried out the window. I
pulled over at a rest stop and considered letting him out, but after
another hour, he stopped crying and fell asleep in the crook of
my arm.† I stroked my thumb over his fish-bone ribs. I pretended
he was the great- or great-great-grandchild of the cat we lost on the
road trip my mother, my father, my sister, and I had taken to the
reservation when I was a girl. I named him Miss. Always missing.‡
Every time I stopped for gas, I gave him extra time to use the litter

---

* March 4, 1995. "Set out from Tallahassee. We slept in the van. That night, a cop
scared the shit out of us becuz we had to move."

† "We still cruising through Alabama, Mississippi, Louisiana."

‡ March 5, 1995. At the top of the entry, my mother crosses out the line "I'm off
will be spending it with the girls." Behind these words, she writes only: not! In
the revised entry, she writes, "This morning I woke up thinking of Dundee. And
were off what a trip through Texas."

box and eat.* Outside Dallas, I detoured to Petco and bought him a
carrier and a toy mouse on a wire to chase in the footwell. I texted
my aunt and warned her I had picked up a stray kitten. I was supposed to stay with her on my return, for a three-day weaving class
in Gallup, but I told her I could find another place to stay. She told
me not to worry and that she would see me soon. We stopped in
Lubbock, where Nathan had moved, though he was out of state for
fieldwork. He told me where to find the key and asked me to feed
Goob, who growled at the kitten under the bedroom door.† The
next morning, we left for our last leg of the trip through New Mexico.‡ The kitten fell asleep in the sun on the dashboard.

* "And were off what a trip through Texas. First through Houston then Dallas
after that straight up to Amarillo."

† "We wanted a beer that evening but we kept hitting dry counties. Boy was he
upset."

‡ "then we reach New Mexico about 8:00 P.M. and we stopped at a convenience
store for beer but no sale in New M 00 we got a room went to dinner then to
bed."

[Cat Killer]

MY COUSIN-SISTER FELL in love with the kitten. She whirled the mouse around and around above his head, and we laughed as he tumbled around the living room floor. My aunt complained and told her not to pick him up—it would be bad for the baby; according to tradition, it was dangerous to handle animals during pregnancy.

That night, while my aunt drank alone in the living room, my cousin-sister and I lay together in bed and talked behind the closed door while Miss chased our fingers, wiggling under the sheets.

"We need to keep him away from my mom," my cousin-sister said.

I asked her why.

"I used to call her a cat killer," she whispered, scandalously. She told me she had had a kitten when she was younger, but her mother begged to let the kitten sleep with her. The next morning, my cousin-sister found the kitten dead, likely smothered, in her mother's bed. She picked up Miss and waggled him in her hands. "We have to watch out for you!" she laughed.

Though it was barely past eight, my aunt suddenly barged in the room and told me to leave my cousin-sister alone. "She's pregnant!" she yelled. "She needs her sleep!" And before I even had time to get up, she slammed off the light switch.

My cousin-sister giggled nervously in the dark.

I told her goodnight and walked into the living room and sat opposite my aunt. We stared at the television screen and did not talk.

* * *

I LEFT FOR Gallup early the next morning; I had enrolled in a three-day Navajo weaving workshop run by Mary Walker out of the Richardson Trading Post. My cousin offered to watch my kitten while I was gone.

The first day was full of introductions. I was surprised that all of the women taking the workshop were white, like Mary, though her fellow instructors—Jennie Slick and Lori Begay—were Navajo.

Jennie sat beside me. She asked me where my family was from. By some brilliant and beautiful chance, Jennie was familiar with my great-grandmother—Jennie's mother had also lived in Sanders, and the two of them had been friends.

"She was very traditional," Jennie told me, about my great-grandmother.

When Lori heard, she smiled. "It was given to you," she said of weaving. "That means you will pick it up quick!"

By the end of the day, we finished building the warps on our looms, though we had only enough time to weave a few rows.

When I returned to my aunt's house, my cousin-sister told me she had given the kitten a bath. His fur was clean and soft and smelled faintly like dish soap. She had found a tick, fat and ugly, under his fur, but her boyfriend had picked it off.

My aunt was angry when she found out. She repeated again that handling him was dangerous for her baby.

My cousin-sister and I sat close together and googled other Navajo superstitions: If you tie knots while pregnant, you will have a hard labor; if you yell at a pregnant woman, the baby will be deaf; if you peel potatoes while pregnant, your baby will have a flat face.

"I can't peel potatoes anymore, Mom," my cousin-sister yelled jokingly to her mother.

My aunt glared at me and scoffed. "I never heard that."

I tried to avoid her eyes.

In the middle of the night, I woke abruptly to a sudden weight on my chest. My aunt had dropped the carrier onto me; I watched her zip him inside. "Leave him in there," my aunt commanded. Sometime later, I woke again after he wedged the point of his nose between the zippers and wiggled his way free. Before I could react, he curled up like a stole around my neck and fell back asleep. He slept there until morning, when I left to weave.

WEAVING A NAVAJO rug requires mastery over the tension of your wool. Each time Jennie visited my loom, she pressed valleys into my thread and warned me not to weave so tight. I remembered when my grandmother had tried to teach me how to crochet: The yarn felt like it was slipping through my fingers, so I overreacted, pulling the yarn too tight. By the end, I could barely fit the hook through a stitch. Each time Jennie visited my loom, she corrected me, but the walls of my rug caved steadily in.

NEITHER MY COUSIN nor my kitten were home when I returned, but a few minutes after I arrived, one of the neighbors knocked on the door. Miss dangled from his hands. "She really chased my two cats around!" he laughed. "They needed it, too. They're both fat."

I accepted Miss into my hands and let him climb onto my shoulder. "He's a boy," I said.

"That's not a boy," he insisted.

I was too tired to argue. I thanked him and closed the door. I walked across the room and set Miss down on the couch, and then I began packing my things. I was angry—with myself for overstaying my welcome, but also with my aunt. I was not the daughter, and she was not the mother, that either of us wanted.

I apologized to Mary Walker, but told her I needed to leave. Understanding, she told me not to worry, that I would always be welcome back.

[Dumpster]

⚜

IN TUCSON, WHILE taking out the trash one morning, I witnessed a temporal fracture, the narrative of my life unraveling into two separate timelines. In one, I watched my friend walk down the sidewalk toward my apartment. We were heading to a breakfast meeting with two editors, and I had offered to give her a ride. A homeless man staggered behind her and seemed to call out to her. She held her eyes on her phone and stepped away from him and into the street.

In the second timeline, I watched my father stagger down the sidewalk toward my apartment. We hadn't spoken in weeks, and I was surprised to see him. A woman walked some distance ahead of him and seemed preoccupied with her phone. He stretched his hand forward and called out to her, but when she lengthened the distance between them, he dropped his eyes to the ground.

I hurried across the lot and stopped on the sidewalk, some middle distance between my friend and my father, and told her I needed a minute. "That's my dad," I said, as if those three words could reconcile this moment for her, or for me, or for him.

My father walked with an obvious limp. His head hung as heavy as the black bag in his hand. I took his bag and we walked, slow and quiet, toward my apartment door. My father told me someone attacked him; the blood bloomed around his eye. The man had kicked him repeatedly in the side. I set his bag in the living room and helped him onto the couch. He fell asleep before I even closed the door.

Later, I found court documents in my father's bag: a record of domestic assault and a mandate to attend domestic violence classes. I folded the documents back into their envelope and slid the envelope back inside his bag.

My father and his girlfriend got back together, even after she called me to ask if he had ever hurt us girls.

I told her he had. I remembered the way he had pinned my sister by the throat to the ground. But I didn't need to elaborate.

"Oh god," she said, filling in my affirmation with her own memories. "Oh god."

"You should leave him," I told her. "He's never going to change."

"But I love him," she said. "I love him."

I fell quiet. There wasn't anything I could say that would convince her to leave.

Weeks later, they moved to California together. There, she finally did leave him after he hurt her again. A new court placed him on probation and mandated he take domestic violence classes.

My father sent me pictures from his life in San Jose: the portable trailers where the homeless could shower; ride-share bikes discarded in piles on the side of the road; picnic tables arranged in the sand and the sun. He captioned the last photograph: "This may be the hardest year of my life."

[Correspondence]

❧

AFTER MY MOTHER'S memorial service, a man who knew her begins emailing me. My aunt has given him my address. He tells me the Lees were like his second family and that one of my uncles was his closest friend.

He describes my mother as "the intellectual one"; as "exceptionally bright." She was academic, always reading. He pictures her with books folded under her arms. "Studying was your mother's world," he writes. "It was as if she found solace in this lone world of hers." When I forward the email to Marie, she responds: *Oh gosh. Sounds like a description of you almost . . .*

He tells me that one time, she and her brother got into a fight. He knocked her books out of her arms, but she didn't fight back. She cried, picked up her books, and carried on her way.

He tells me her parents were abusive. They drank. He thought my mother wanted a life away from what she went through growing up.

He tells me to let him know when I plan to visit the reservation; he tells me he has more to share. I never do. I am afraid of the girl he knew—knowing, myself, where she would go.

A few months after we begin corresponding, my aunt calls and asks if I am still speaking to him. I tell her I am. "He's a liar," she warns me. "Don't listen to anything he says."

[Changing Woman]

TWO MONTHS LATER, at the end of the summer, I enrolled in another weaving workshop in Window Rock. I rented a room in town instead of staying with my aunt.

My cousin-sister had her baby a few weeks earlier; she was the tiniest little girl.

I attended classes between running errands: driving my cousin to her neonatal appointments, to the laundromat in Fort Defiance, to the Walmart in Gallup to buy a breast pump and diapers and a new car seat. I skipped the weaving field trips the other women took to Canyon de Chelly and the Hubbell Trading Post so I could spend time with my niece, who was precious, a thing I couldn't let go.

Because the workshop was being held at the hotel and not at Richardson, I was able to weave after dinner and late into the night. I wove obsessively, single-mindedly, as I so often lived my life. I knew there were stories of women falling sick from weaving in excess, and taboos about weaving at night, but I was determined to finish my rug before I left at the end of the week. In my exhaustion, I missed counts: My weft skipped over warp threads, and the lines of my design grew crooked.

My aunt asked to see pictures of my progress, but when I showed her the partially finished rug, she squinted and asked what the design meant.

"I don't know," I said. "I'm just practicing." Mary Walker had told us to consider our first project as a sampler, a way to hone our technique.

"It should tell a story," my aunt insisted, and she pointed at the top of the rug, where the bare bones of the warp still showed through. "This could be the sky," she said, and then she pointed at the squash blossom set against blue. "And that could be the sun."

I told her I would think about it.

ONE LATE AFTERNOON, I visited one of my grandmothers in Sanders. She drove me around my family's allotment, and she took me to visit Pauline Tom's house, where one of my grandfathers still lived. Water collected in a deep, muddy pool in the front yard. We entered through the back. A dusty, blinking kitten cleaned his paw in front of the door, overlooking the water. The house, three small rooms, smelled like a litter box.

"She raised eight kids here," my grandmother said.

We drove up the road to visit another grandmother, and when I showed them a picture of my rug, her husband chuckled. "That's not a Navajo design," he said, knowingly; his cousin was Barbara Teller, he said, and he would know.

I assured them I knew, that I was just practicing. For the rest of the visit, they talked around and over my head.

We returned to my grandmother's trailer, and while she made dinner, I walked down her dirt road toward the river. A white dog followed me. I walked past a pink trailer and an old corral. The grass was tall and yellow. I found an empty wash, then turned around and walked back. As I walked toward the front door, a rufous hummingbird buzzed away from her feeder.

We sat on her couch and ate spaghetti with garlic bread, and she told me about my cousin's kinaaldá, which had been held at her house a few weeks before. Women from all branches of our family had gathered around my grandmothers' shade. They leaned thin boards of wood against its poles to build a makeshift hogan. My cousin ran in the morning with her sisters and brothers, and my grandmothers smiled, recalling their laughter. Then they lay my cousin out on a Pendleton blanket and massaged her entire body. They lined a pit, dug into the ground at the center of the hogan, with corn husks, and she mixed the cake over the warm coals. My grandmothers were there throughout the ceremony, to guide her. "She did such a good job," my grandmother said, "and the kinaaldá is so important. It gives these girls a sense of worth, a sense of pride."

Before I left, she dug inside her fridge and cut a thin wedge from the cake's heart. She wrapped it in aluminum foil and handed it to me. "You have so much to learn," my grandmother said, pressing the package into my hands.

AFTER MY MOTHER'S memorial service, as we drove back to my grandmother's house, my cousin-sister had pointed over my shoulder, out the window, at the steppe and the mesas beyond the road. "That's where I ran for my kinaaldá," she said.

"Your what?" I had asked, startled by the word I didn't recognize.

"Her key-naal-dah," my aunt repeated, stressing each syllable. "Her puberty ceremony."

My mind flashed suddenly to an entry I had read in my mother's diary, about my cousin-sister: The entry declared she was on the rag. I hadn't known who she was then. I flipped through her diaries looking for a mention of my period and felt an acute sense of jealousy when I didn't find anything.

"She did the entire ceremony herself," my aunt said, glowing.

My eyes locked on to the edge of pink stone and blue sky. "I never did anything like that," I said, remembering the way I had tried to conceal my first period from my grandmother and Fran.

My aunt sighed. "Didn't your mom teach you nothing?"

Once we were home, my aunt gave me a picture book: *Kinaaldá: A Navajo Girl Grows Up*. The book tells the story of the *first* kinaaldá, which is the story of Changing Woman. In the story, First Man found a baby girl one morning at dawn, and he and First Woman raised her under the direction of the Holy People. This girl was Changing Woman, who was named for the speed at which she grew—for each day, she grew a year, and at the end of twelve days, she reached puberty. The Holy People held the first kinaaldá to mark her transformation. In the Navajo creation stories, Changing Woman is Mother; is Earth; is fertility; is time. As the seasons pass, she ages—an old woman in winter, born again each spring. She birthed the people, the Diné, by rubbing excess skin from her arms and breasts. She created the four original clans and gave the people the blessingway: rites and prayers of healing, creation, harmony, and peace.

My great-grandmother, Pauline Tom, was very traditional. She knew the ways. She knew the stories and the ceremonies. She tried to teach my grandmothers, and they tried to teach my mothers, and they tried to teach their daughters, but not everyone listened or cared.

Later that night, in the dark, my cousin-sister told me her mother disappeared from her kinaaldá, that her grandmothers were not there.

"Where was your mom?" I asked.

"Oh," she sighed, an exaggerated sigh that masked a laugh. "She was just off with some *man*."

I STRUGGLED WITH the final, long inch of my rug, which required a different, smaller set of tools. Instead of cedar, the weavers adapted the thin metal wire they stripped out of an old umbrella to use as a batten. The last few rows were woven using a tapestry needle. My back and shoulders ached, but I was determined to finish.

I noticed Lori watching me, and when I caught her eye, she smiled. "Nizhóní," she said. Beautiful.

Before I even finished my rug, Jennie prepared a new warp for me to weave at home. Then she helped me take my finished rug off the loom. I gave the rug to my cousin-sister before I left.

I drove six hours home in the dark. Once home, I dug around the kitchen until I remembered the cake my grandmother had given me. I pulled it out of my bag and ate it with my hands. The cake was moist and dense and gritty, and just a little bit sweet.

[Selvage]

DURING THE LAST short weeks of summer, I met someone playing a videogame. He lived in Canada, but after we started talking,
he booked a flight to visit me in Tucson. He spent ten days with me.

I wanted to take him hiking, but the Tucson summer was too
hot for him, so we spent most of those days sharing our favorite
things with each other: We binge-watched an entire season of
RuPaul's Drag Race, and we played through the beginning of *Dark
Souls*, and on the long drive to the reservation, we listened to Terry
Pratchett's *The Wee Free Men*.

I wanted him to meet my cousin-sister and my niece, a lima bean
in his hands. I wanted to show him the pink mesas and the red clay
and the sagebrush that flowered yellow. "It's beautiful," he said.

We drove my cousin-sister to pick up dinner, and she told us
quiet, sad stories from the back seat. When we returned to the
house, my aunt pressed my new boyfriend to take shots with her,
but he declined. My cousin-brother and his girlfriend turned up,
and they started grilling steaks in the backyard. The girlfriend swat-
ted at a small dog with a broom, and I could feel him tense beside
me. He grew quieter and quieter the longer we stayed, and I told
him we could leave.

We rented a room and lay in bed facing each other. The tears
collected in our eyes. He understood all the ways I wished that
place could be; I understood if I wanted to be whole, I would never
be able to stay.

A few weeks after he returned home, he asked me to marry him.
I said yes.

In November, I visited him in Toronto, where I met his family for the first time. I brought Miss with me, and he stayed in Toronto, to live with my future mother-in-law. My future husband lived an hour and a half outside Toronto, in a place called Kitchener-Waterloo. We spent most days at his rented office space, where he tutored high school and university students in physics and chemistry. I graded papers in the lobby.

The town and the landscape reminded me of Pennsylvania. One evening after work, we passed an Amish horse and buggy on the road.

His stepmother helped us plan the wedding, which was held at a country club. When Owen first suggested it, I had laughed hysterically, and then begun to cry. I didn't belong there, I told him. But the club was one originally founded by the Jewish families who couldn't get into the usual country clubs; its charter mandated a diverse membership. Before I left for Tucson, we toured the venue. His father handed us a packet when we arrived, complete with possible table arrangements, hors d'oeuvres, and the menu. We ruled out a walking down the aisle, a giving away, and a first dance. I felt less nervous about what I was getting into.

The wedding was less than six weeks away.

MY COUSIN-SISTER, CRYING, called me a few days later. She asked if she could stay with me for a while. She and my aunt were still fighting, and she didn't feel safe. Immediately, I answered yes.

I drove up to get her the next day. We weren't able to fit everything—her clothes, the baby's clothes, her toys, her Pack 'n Play—but we fit all that we could.

My aunt tried to weave a different narrative of events, but she didn't try to stop us from leaving.

My cousin-sister and her baby stayed with me for more than a month. The three of us slept together in my bed; we swaddled my niece and carefully tucked her between us at night.

My cousin-sister became friends with one of my downstairs

neighbors, a woman with two children of her own. I had never spoken to my neighbor, any of my neighbors, in the years I had lived
there. My cousin-sister and the neighbor went for long walks during the day.

I tried to talk with my cousin-sister about her and her daughter's
future. She wanted to be a florist, to own her own business one day.
I tried to help her imagine a life away from her mother. I tried to
imagine the ways I might help.

I convinced her to attend an Al-Anon meeting, a program similar to AA, but for the families of alcoholics, this one specifically for
adult children of alcoholics. I had been meaning to go to one for
years, but I had never worked up the courage to go alone. We
tucked my niece into her car seat and arrived at the church early.
We loitered at the edge of the parking lot, and I noticed an explo-
sion of feathers beneath a mesquite tree where a hawk must have
made a snack of a dove.

A meeting is a difficult place for a baby. She fussed and then exploded, pale brown down her legs. My cousin-sister ducked out of
the meeting but signaled me to stay. I listened to the others talk
about isolation, and I began to cry. My cousin-sister did not return,
so before the meeting concluded, I excused myself after her. Her
daughter was still crying, and I offered to drive us home. In the car,
she told me she had hoped to hear what they said, and I tried to
explain what I had heard, but that didn't feel like enough.

My aunt called me night after night to yell. She told me to get rid
of my cats, which she called filthy; she claimed they would hurt my
niece. She threatened to call CPS. She yelled about her grandbaby,
her grandbaby, her grandbaby. One morning, my cousin-sister and
I jokingly pressed the tips of our fingers to the baby's lips each
time she cried and whispered, "Shh, shh, shh." That night, my aunt
called and yelled at me to never cover her grandbaby's mouth. I felt
a chill run through my body. How had she known? *She practices
black magic,* my mother had said.

I found out later my cousin-sister had mentioned the joke to her friend, who told my cousin-brother's girlfriend, who told her mother. The information carried by mouth, not by magic. But I could not shake the feeling that my aunt's eyes were always watching us.

I tried to convince my cousin-sister to stay in my apartment after I moved out, but she applied for housing assistance on the reservation and received good news. Before I left for Canada for my wedding, I drove her to Phoenix, to stay with a friend until her new home was ready to move into.

WE MARRIED IN January, a few days after the New Year. His mother made the skirt and the blouse I wore. The night before the ceremony, we stayed with his father and his stepmother, who left me a card on the nightstand. "Like you, my mother was not alive to see me marry my soulmate," she wrote, "and I know how difficult this might be for you." She gifted me one of her mother's handkerchiefs, which she had carried on her own wedding day.

The next morning, we drove to Kitchener, to our new apartment, empty except for two desks, a chair, and a mattress on the floor. I let my cat out of her carrier, and she bolted around the living room and then into the kitchen, where she hid in a cupboard above the fridge.

My words feel inadequate. I had never felt that kind of love, but I have never learned how to write about happiness.

TWO WEEKS LATER, I flew back to Tucson to finish packing my things. Three of my oldest friends were flying out for the Tucson version of our wedding celebration, which we started calling the "great wedding bird adventure," and my sister Eileen flew out a few days early to visit me.

When I first told her about my wedding plans, she told me she intended to go to rehab, to try and get clean, but she was still using when she arrived. On the drive to the reservation, she pulled a shawl over her head in the passenger seat to hide the act of sliding a needle into her arm—not from me, but from anyone who might have glanced down into the car. I said nothing and stared at the road. She fell asleep with her shawl draped across her chest.

We stopped to meet our cousin-sister and our niece, and then we visited a trading post, where we each bought a turquoise ring. We planned to visit one of our grandmothers, but first she begged me to take her to visit our aunt. When I told her no, she started yelling at me: how it wasn't fair; how she deserved to meet her family; how she wouldn't have come if she knew I was going to be such a bitch.

I relented. I drove her to our aunt's, but parked at the end of the street. I didn't want my aunt to see my car parked outside, even though I knew she would know I was there. I asked Eileen not to be long. I watched her weave down the rutted road, up our grandmother's driveway, and knock on the front door. I thought of all the times my aunt and my cousin-sister had ignored those front-door knocks, the uncomfortable hush that fell as they waited for the unexpected visitor to leave, but to my surprise, the door opened and my sister disappeared inside.

An hour later, I was still waiting, and our grandmother would be waiting, so I got out of the car and walked to the house.

My aunt answered the door with an apology. "I was drunk," she said, as if that could erase the things she said. It was the kind of apology I had lost all patience for.

I told Eileen it was time to go.

In the car, we started screaming at each other again. "I've hurt people, too," Eileen yelled. "I'm a shitty person. But I'm not going to *judge* her. Like, who the fuck am I?"

I understood why Eileen wanted to meet our aunt—why she identified with her. I was wrong to try and keep them apart, but I wasn't ready to admit that to her yet.

The argument shifted, and she told me I was stupid to marry a man I had just met. It wasn't possible for me to know him. And when I tried to tell her what I loved about him—our shared world-view, the things we wanted out of life—she told me my version of love wasn't love. She told me love should be passionate, full of fireworks. She told me I had never loved her, that I always chose my father over her. I tried to explain that I took care of him so she didn't have to, that I took care of him out of love for them both. It was a crazy thing, to be screaming about love.

We met our grandmother in a parking lot; she was on her way to a basketball game. My sister and I were both full of smiles and hugs and laughter, like magic, as if we had not been screaming moments before.

When we were on the road again, Eileen slept. She woke as we neared Tucson. She asked me to take her to a park to look for dope, but I refused, and my refusal turned into another argument.

Back in the apartment, I hid in my room and listened to her complain loudly on the phone with her boyfriend about what different people we were.

MY FRIENDS ARRIVED, one by one. They shared an Airbnb on the north side of town. I cooked two pots of chili and brought them over with a cat puzzle. We pushed pieces of brown and black and gray around the table, and my friend's boyfriend complained I wouldn't let anyone consult the box, which I considered cheating.

The next day, we carpooled to Willcox to see the wintering sandhill cranes. We hiked onto the playa as the sun set and waited for the birds to arrive. At first, they were pin-sized silhouettes above the mountains, but as twilight descended, they ventured closer, glints of silver in the crowded dark. They formed a burbling chorus above our heads. We could hear them shouting still as we walked back to our cars.

Three days later, my husband and I packed my life inside my two-door Yaris: a suitcase of clothes, two boxes of books, and a box of my childhood toys. I packed a box of letters from my father and sister, and a box of photographs, and also the box of my mother's things. Everything else I sold or gave away.

★ ★ ★

MY FIRST WINTER in Canada was difficult. "Life has been good here," I wrote in an email to Marie, "but I've cried a lot this week." I missed Tucson. I missed my friends. I missed the sun and the birds and the cacti. I missed the desert, and I missed the mountains. I missed the smell of the earth, and I missed the smell of the rain. This longing surfaced often, without warning, and each time I retreated further inside myself.

A dog barked too loudly upstairs. The neighbor, a man with an assault rifle tattooed across his back, made me nervous. I watched him out the window. He built and demolished and rebuilt a tree house in the backyard, though I never saw a child in it. One night, after a branch splintered in a storm, he climbed into the tree in the rain and used a circular saw to try to cut it down. One day, a woman walked into the yard holding a drink in one hand. They started arguing, and I watched her try to wrestle a hammer out of his hand. I did not want to watch, but I could not look away.

Owen questioned, often, if I was happy. I was not always, but I felt closer to happy than I had ever been.

EILEEN CALLS TO tell me she is clean. She met a boy online playing *PUBG Mobile*, and they fell into a quick kind of love. She moved with him to his parents' house, somewhere in rural Ohio. She calls me on a walk and asks me to identify a bird. She tells me she is happy; she tells me she is loved.

She calls me, crying, when he gets angry and controlling. She wants to leave, but she tells me she has nowhere to go.

She calls me and says she is back in Pittsburgh.

She calls me and says she is moving in with her best friend, who teaches yoga in West Virginia. From there, she calls me less often. She sends me photos of a daycare her friend is renovating; Eileen helps them paint the shelves and tables primary shades of red, blue, and yellow.

She calls and tells me she has started painting again. She sends me pictures of her works-in-progress: marbled lines of turquoise and luminescent swirls of shell. She starts livestreaming her painting sessions on Facebook, and I watch her paint a slice of pepperoni pizza, which floats in a cloudy blue sky. She sits cross-legged on the floor and paints a cow skull surrounded by two button cacti and a crushed beer can.

She starts saving for her own place; she starts saving for a lawyer, to change the custody agreement for her son.

She starts dating a tattoo artist. She calls me crying because his anxieties feed into her own. She tells me she has lost more than twenty pounds. She is always anxious. She tells me there is something broken inside him. "I can see it in his eyes," she says, and I know it's these broken eyes that hold her to him, this man who reminds me too much of our father. Eileen wants to take-care of him, like our mother would.

She calls me as she walks, block after block, because her boyfriend would not give her a ride. She tells me she found an apartment, but she doesn't have enough for the deposit. I can hear the city behind her: a car door slamming and two men's voices, loud but indistinct. She passes her favorite bar and starts negotiating a drink with herself—she just wants one before her shift. I try to talk her out of it. I tell her to schedule a time to have a drink later, after she has the apartment nailed down. She walks into the bar and I tell her to order a Sprite instead. She tells me she loves me and hangs up.

She messages me a few minutes later and says she didn't have time to drink; she's late for work. The "lol" at the end of the message is desperate and full of grief.

She messages me a few hours later to tell me the apartment fell through. I offer to help her start looking for a new place while she is at work, but then she messages me from the backroom of the convenience store where she works. "I can't stop crying," she tells me. "How do I stop crying?" I tell her to breathe, as deeply as she can; to fill up the bottoms of her lungs. She tells me she *is* breathing, that it doesn't work. Instead of telling her to think of something happy, I tell her it helps me to think about something that makes me happy-sad. It's easier to stop those kinds of tears. I tell her I think about Don. I try to remind her of his orange boat. The smell of his van. The fishing poles that rattled above our heads. The time the four of us motored out to a little mangrove island and found hermit crabs poking around on the shore. She tells me she remembers the time he stopped to move a turtle across the road, and then she stops messaging me.

WHEN MY SISTER and I were little, my grandmother told us to pray for our father to "be sober," as if God could magically shift our father into another state of being, a state of sobriety; as if sobriety did not necessitate some shift in thought or in action by our father himself.

My father sends me an email from California. *Law enforcement is on the way,* he writes. *Please forgive me.*

I don't respond. I don't hear from him again for weeks. I search his name on VINELink, a victim notification network, and locate his inmate number.

I consider writing him a letter, but I don't.

I cannot forgive my father; forgiveness risks too much. My mother chose my father, and men like him, and I must make another choice. I must choose my sisters.

IN MAY, I heard about a Navajo weaving workshop that would be taught by Lynda Teller Pete and Barbara Teller Ornelas in Toronto, at the upcoming Indigenous Fashion Week. I had wanted to take a class with them for years, but the timing had never been right. My husband enrolled me in the class as a birthday gift.

I stayed with my mother-in-law during the class and took the bus and the train into the city. The bus route was one of the strangest I had ever been on—it wove through a garden and a neighborhood full of mansions, with front gates and driveways full of expensive cars. The bus was always empty.

I got lost trying to navigate the city. Google Maps told me to use a network of underground pedestrian tunnels called the PATH, in all caps, but I kept losing my way. I asked a man on the street for directions and, like a trickster in an urban fantasy, he said, "Take any door and you will find it."

I turned around and walked into a terminal with door after numbered door.

I found the building by what felt like a miracle. Before class, I spotted Barbara and Lynda outside; Barbara wearing a black-and-red biil—a traditional Navajo dress—and Linda wearing a crushed velvet shirt.

I listened closely as they introduced themselves in Navajo; I recognized my grandfather's clan.

"My grandfather's clan was Tábąąhá, too," I said, when it came time to introduce myself.

Lynda gasped and clapped her hands. "We're nálís!" Grandmothers, she said excitedly, in the Navajo way.

It had been almost a year since the last time I wove, but I picked it up again fast. I asked Lynda to teach me how to create diagonal designs, and she helped me count out my rows.

At the end of the last day, they held a special ceremony to trim our rugs' selvage cords, the braided threads that look like tassels at a rug's four corners. They told us the selvage cords were like the rug's umbilical cord, and that, traditionally, Navajos bury a baby's umbilical cord in the earth, so their children will always recognize home.

We cut our cords one by one, their hands guiding ours. When it was my turn, they called me "granddaughter," as if welcoming me into their family. Barbara closed my hand around the ends of wool, and as I walked away, I slid them into my pocket. I considered bringing them with me to Tucson the next time I visited, to pat beneath the sand, but then I remembered the new home I was trying to build. It was difficult for me to believe a few bits of string could make a place feel like home, but when I returned to the apartment my husband and I shared, I folded the ends of my selvage cords inside the handkerchief my mother-in-law gave me, which I placed inside my mother's carved brown bowl.

happy Mothers where I'm
Day I love sad
you MoMMy.
and I will
always love
you even

TITLE: Handmade Mother's Day card of unknown provenance.

DATE: undated

TYPE OF RESOURCE: personal correspondence

DESCRIPTION: A handmade Mother's Day card on off-white paper. I am not
sure whether my sister Eileen or I made it. Written in green crayon: "happy
Mothers Day I love you MoMMy. and I will always love you even where I'm
sad"

TITLE: Alexandra slides down a metal slide.

DATE: undated

TYPE OF RESOURCE: color photographs

DESCRIPTION: Lee's daughter Alexandra on a slide in a park. She is bundled in a winter coat. She appears frozen in the eye of the camera; the world blurs around her.

TITLE: Mike, Fran, Thomas, Marty, and Lee pose for a group photo.

DATE: 1995

TYPE OF RESOURCE: color negatives

DESCRIPTION: My parents and their partners pose for a photograph near a grill built of cinder blocks and concrete. My father's friend Thomas, whom my father once saved from an electrical shock delivered by the internal components of a microwave, stands in the center.

TITLE: Lee and Fran flash their breasts at the camera.

DATE: 1995

TYPE OF RESOURCE: color negatives

DESCRIPTION: Smiling, my mother and Fran stand outside their home and flash their breasts at the camera.

TITLE: Tire tracks in the dirt.

DATE: 1995

TYPE OF RESOURCE: color negatives

DIGITAL ORIGIN: reformatted digital

DESCRIPTION: Evidence from other photographs in my mother's collection suggests this was not an accidental exposure but an intentionally captured image of light, shadow, and earth.

TITLE: Lee poses with her daughters Eileen and Danielle.

DATE: 1995

TYPE OF RESOURCE: color negatives

DESCRIPTION: My sister and I pose with our mother in the front yard of the house off Military Trail.

ACKNOWLEDGMENTS

THANK YOU TO the University of Arizona Creative Writing MFA for providing time, space, and community. Thank you especially to Ander Monson and Alison Hawthorne Deming, whose support and guidance have shaped my writing practice forever.

Thank you to my workshop colleagues for your early and formative feedback: Abby Dockter, Thomas Dai, Emily Maloney, Janet Towle, Peyton Prater-Stark, Clare McClane, Miranda Trimmier, and Kathryn Gougelet.

Thank you to my writing teachers from another life: Catherine Dent, Kazim Ali, and Kim Van Alkemade, who provided me endless opportunities at Ship and beyond. Special thanks to Kim, who read and offered feedback on the very first draft of this book. Your ongoing support has meant everything to me.

Thank you to my teachers at GrubStreet: Rita Zoey Chin and Jennifer De Leon.

Thank you also to Katherine Wisser and Donna Webber, who introduced me to the world of libraries and archives at Simmons College.

Thank you to my weaving teachers: Mary Walker, Jennie Slick, Lori Begay, Barbara Teller Ornelas, and Lynda Teller Pete. You have given me another language with which to speak.

Thank you to the Rona Jaffe Foundation, whose support came at a critical time in my career as a writer. Everything began that summer of 2016!

Thank you to my agents, Jessica Friedman and Alexandra Christie, for ushering my work into the world.

Thank you to the editors and publishers who have offered feedback and guidance on the work that surfaced alongside this project: the editors at *Brevity*, who selected my essay "Blood; Quantum" as the winner of their student contest; Margot Kahn and Kelly McMasters, who published "Annotating the First Page of the First Navajo-English Dictionary" in their anthology *This Is the Place;* and the editors at *The New Yorker*, who excerpted my work on their platform.

Thank you to Jack Jones Literary Arts for inviting me into their cohort of 2018 fellows, whose work was inspiring and invigorating. Thank you also to Natalie Diaz for providing me the opportunity to attend.

My love and thanks to my editor Nicole Counts. I would not have made it to the end of this book without you.

My love and thanks also to Marie Hathaway for editorial support on so many early drafts. I don't feel I have the right words to thank you for your love and friendship over the years, but I hope we can sit somewhere and cry together soon.

And finally, my love and thanks to my husband, Owen, who kept me fed and watered through the last long days of this book.

DANIELLE GELLER is a writer of personal essays and memoir. Her first book, *Dog Flowers,* was published by One World/Penguin Random House in 2021. She received her MFA in creative writing for nonfiction at the University of Arizona, and a Rona Jaffe Writers' Award in 2016. Her work has appeared in *The Paris Review, The New Yorker, Brevity,* and *Arizona Highways,* and has been anthologized in *This Is the Place.* She lives with her husband and two cats in British Columbia, where she teaches creative writing at the University of Victoria. She is also a faculty mentor for the low-residency MFA program at the Institute of American Indian Arts. She is a member of the Navajo Nation: born to the Tsi'naajinii, born for the white man.

DANIELLEGELLER.COM

TWITTER: @DELLEGELLER

INSTAGRAM: @DELLEGELLER